371.3078

MASON

OMAGH COLLEGE LIBRARY

OC

D0303647

...rn on or before the last date stamped below.

Using Communications Media in Open and Flexible Learning

CXO 0012649 3B

1120977

Open and Distance Learning Series

Series Editor: Fred Lockwood

Activities in Self-Instructional Text Fred Lockwood
Exploring Open and Distance Learning Derek Rowntree
Improving Your Students' Learning Alistair Morgan
Key Terms and Issues in Open and Distance Learning Barbara Hodgson
Programme Evaluation and Quality Judith Calder
Using Communications Media in Open and Flexible Learning Robin Mason

-1 MAR 1999

OPEN AND DISTANCE LEARNING SERIES

Using Communications Media in Open and Flexible Learning

ROBIN MASON

KOGAN PAGE
Published in association with the
Institute of Educational Technology, Open University

1120977

First published in 1994

Reprinted 1998

Apart from any fair dealing for the purposes of research or private study, or criticism or review, as permitted under the Copyright, Designs and Patents Act, 1988, this publication may only be reproduced, stored or transmitted, in any form or by any means, with the prior permission in writing of the publishers, or in the case of reprographic reproduction in accordance with the terms of licences issued by the Copyright Licensing Agency. Enquiries concerning reproduction outside those terms should be sent to the publishers at the undermentioned address:

Kogan Page Limited
120 Pentonville Road
London N1 9JN

© Robin Mason, 1994

British Library Cataloguing in Publication Data

A CIP record for this book is available from the British Library.

ISBN 0 7494 1149 X

Typeset by BookEns Ltd, Baldock, Herts.
Printed and bound in Great Britain by
Antony Rowe Ltd, Chippenham, Wiltshire

-1 MAR 1999

Contents

Series editor's foreword

The use of open and distance learning is increasing dramatically in all sections of education and training. This increase is occurring both in the UK and around the world. Many schools, colleges, universities, companies and organizations are already using open and distance learning practices in their teaching and training and want to develop these further. Furthermore, many individuals have heard about open and distance learning and would welcome the opportunity to find out more about it and explore its potential.

Whatever your current interest in open and distance learning and experience within it, I believe there will be something in this series of short books for you. The series is directed at teachers, trainers, educational advisers, in-house training managers and training consultants involved in designing open and distance learning systems and materials. It will be invaluable for those working in learning environments ranging from industry and commerce to public sector organizations, from schools and colleges to universities.

This series is designed to provide a comprehensive coverage of the field of open and distance learning. Each title focuses on a different aspect of designing and developing open and distance learning and provides concrete advice and information, which is built upon current theory and research in the field and how it relates to actual practice.

This basis of theory, research and development experience is unique in the area of open and distance learning. I say this with some confidence since the Open University Institute of Educational Technology, from which virtually all the authors are drawn, contains the largest collection of educational technologists (course designers, developers and researchers) in the world. Since the inception of the Open University in 1969, members of the Institute have made a major contribution to the design and production of learning systems and materials not just in the Open University but in many other organizations in this country and elsewhere. We would now like to share our experience and findings with you.

In this book, *Using Communications Media in Open and Flexible Learning*, Robin Mason presents a readable and informative account of the educational uses of three interactive technologies: computer conferencing, audiographics and video conferencing. The early chapters introduce the issues for students, teachers and organizations considering courses and training programmes based on these media. What is the educational value of interactivity? What support mechanisms are necessary in using telecommunications? What implications arise from asynchronous media?

From her considerable experience and research in the field of telecommunications media, the author has chosen nine case studies from around the world which illustrate these issues in practice. Throughout her writing she aims to present a balanced view of these technologies, noting the enthusiasm of the early adopters, as well as the drawbacks and pitfalls of technology-driven solutions to deep educational problems.

This work provides an invaluable introduction to the educational use of communications media for planners, administrators, teachers and trainers. More significantly, it presents a broad-ranging and well-informed assessment of the current application of communications technology in the educational process.

Fred Lockwood

Preface

It is my intention to provide the reader with an easily accessible introduction to the educational uses of three telecommunications technologies: computer conferencing, audiographics and videoconferencing. As these three all involve person-to-person interaction, my bias may be obvious at the outset. I am a proponent of communication in the learning environment. My ideas about this activity are laid out in Chapter 2.

My professional experience has come primarily from distance education at the Open University in the UK. However, I welcome the convergence of distance education and traditional face-to-face teaching, as bringing the stimulus and best features of each to the other. No factor has so contributed to this convergence as the development of the communications technologies.

My aim is to present generalized information about using these technologies and to address issues on a wide spectrum across the major education levels, ages and situations. This very broad treatment is then made specific and practical by a range of case studies which detail an application in a real context. I had hoped to present some 'failures' amongst the case studies, as I think that more can often be learned from others' mistakes than from their successes. However, although some telecommunications courses have certainly been failures, it has proved too difficult to obtain detailed information, or too indelicate to publish it.

I have not included any costings of these media, although I am well aware that cost is a crucial factor in even considering their application. Having been involved myself in a cost study of each of these media, I feel that generalizations about costs are not very useful, and specifics are too dependent on context. However, I have not indulged in what I know are costly recommendations for practices or equipment which may be desirable educationally, but are not realistic financially.

A short annotated bibliography of further reading is provided at the end, and I have tried to select some of the 'standard texts' (if one can use such a term for a field which has hardly any history at all), as well as some unfamiliar works which I feel are worthy of a wider readership.

One of the reasons for writing this book is to bring together information which currently exists in a very wide range of sources. Because the field of educational telecommunications is such a hybrid, relevant literature, research and evaluations are scattered very broadly over such disparate journals, conference proceedings and local guides, that the experienced academic has difficulty keeping track of it all, let alone the newcomer to the scene.

Finally, I have tried to integrate the issues and experiences of users around the world – although this has inevitably been superficial. Nevertheless, as these technologies are at their best when bringing together disparate people, I have felt it necessary to try to present a global picture of their value in education and training.

Chapter 1

Telecommunications Media

What are they?

There are three ways of communicating electronically: writing, speaking and displaying. These translate roughly into text, audio and video. Various media have developed around these modes of communication, but the three chosen for this book are computer conferencing, audiographics and videoconferencing. Although they are fairly distinct in their application and equipment requirements at the current time, the trend is entirely toward their eventual merger into multimedia desktop conferencing. The essence of this book is to present these three media in their distinct forms, to discuss the issues of their use and to give examples of their application in teaching and training contexts. However, the future development of these technologies will also be considered at relevant points in the discussion. As with virtually every new technology, multimedia desktop conferencing is heralded as a revolutionary concept for education. The history of educational development shows us, however, that these 'revolutions' usually turn out to be gradual changes and adjustments. What follows, therefore, is an attempt to facilitate this gradual change by showing how communications media can be accommodated in education and training.

The term 'communications media' is used here, rather than the more familiar 'interactive media', as a way of making a distinction between person-to-person interaction and personal interaction with textual information. This latter category includes computer-based training (CBT), interactive video (CD-I) and CD-ROM, none of which will be covered in this book, although they are often referred to as 'interactive'. So the subject here is, in essence, using electronic technologies to facilitate educational exchanges amongst people – by writing, speaking and listening, and displaying and seeing.

The 'tele' part of telecommunications usually signals the use of the telephone network as the carrier of the communications. However, satellite, cable and microwave radio links can also be used as the means of transmission. To the educational practitioner, the means of transmission is largely irrelevant, just as the long-distance telephone caller is not bothered about whether the call is going via satellite or terrestrial cable.

Computer conferencing, audiographics and videoconferencing can all be used in a range of applications: in primary, secondary and tertiary education; training, vocational and professional fields; large- and small-scale implementations; in traditional campus-based settings and study centres, in the home or the workplace.

Computer conferencing

Communication by written messages, stored in a central location and accessible by a group of users at any time, is the basis of computer conferencing. This medium really has no non-electronic counterpart; it is an amalgam of letter writing, group discussion and newspaper letters-to-the-editor, but very different from any of these individually. It is written interaction, produced and continuously available over time. The ambiguity this creates is both its strength and its weakness. Its educational value is grasped by almost all who try it, but few would claim to have realized its unique potential.

Unlike the other two media discussed in this book, computer conferencing is asynchronous. Teacher and learner can read and enter messages at any time, from any place. Thus the group of users need never 'meet' at the same time, let alone the same place. As we shall see in Chapter 4, which is devoted to this medium, certain caveats must be made to this apparent openness. Nevertheless, it remains true in principle that learner and teacher form an educational environment in a non-existent time and place. This form of unreality has led to the term 'virtual' being applied particularly to the use of computer conferencing in an educational context: virtual classroom, virtual contiguity, virtual learning community.

Audiographics

The medium of audiographics is perhaps the most volatile of the three under discussion, because rapid technological development and lower prices for equipment will soon turn it into multimedia desktop conferencing. Audiographics, as a distinct medium, is most likely to prevail in the primary/secondary sector and possibly in 'traditional' distance education much longer than in professional and training fields. The reasons for this prediction will be discussed in Chapter 5 and will also be evident in the case studies in Chapter 7.

The pure form of audiographics consists of exactly what the name implies: voice and graphics exchange. The graphics – really any still images – are an add-on to what was originally just plain audioconferencing. Telephone tutoring has a long history in distance education in many countries. When several parties are involved in the same conversation, it is called audioconferencing, and requires an audiobridge to handle the various interconnections. With graphics added to the voice connection, a graphics tablet or drawing mechanism is required at each site, and all the users see the same picture on a monitor – hence the term 'screen sharing'.

Various forms of audiographics have been used in education for the last 15 years, usually with purpose-built equipment. In recent years audiographics has been 'put on the personal computer'; that is, the keyboard, monitor and file-sharing mechanisms of the computer can be used to generate and exchange graphics. Now it is possible to use existing software packages and various additional equipment to create an audiographics system without specialist equipment or a tailor-made audiographics software package. Furthermore, it is possible to add a video window (see Figure 1.1), a camera, a built-in microphone and communications software, and the result is multimedia desktop conferencing. As we shall see in Chapter 5, audiographic uses in education and training are still distinct from the very few examples of multimedia desktop conferencing applications currently in practice in the training sector.

The audiographics medium is synchronous: the users gather at their various sites at the same time. It is usually group-based; that is, groups of two to eight share one set of equipment, and up to perhaps six different groups may be interconnected. Each site hears the conversation from any of the other sites and can draw on the shared screen. Essentially it is, therefore, a small group discussion medium.

Videoconferencing

Videoconferencing is more varied in its uses than the other two media: it can be used with large lecture groups of relatively passive students or for

Photo courtesy of VIS-A-VIS

Figure 1.1 *Desktop conferencing with a video window*

multi-site interactive discussions. A lecturer delivering a traditional 'chalk and talk' lecture may have one class present and another, or several others, at a distance. On the other hand, videoconferencing can be used – particularly in training – to transmit a programme consisting of, for example, demonstrations, video segments of material made earlier, discussions amongst experts, and question and answer sessions from participating sites. Consortia of institutions operate videoconferencing courses for continuing education and training involving experts from many sites and students from all over the country. At the other end of the spectrum, rural or isolated education centres use videoconferencing to access courses from a host institution. The range of uses is very wide.

While the primary uses of computer conferencing and audiographics are educational, videoconferencing has until recently been a largely business tool, used for small group interactions. Currently, however, the education and training market is the major growth area for videoconferencing equipment.

The equipment for videoconferencing was designed originally for a specially prepared room with microphones, cameras, monitors and soundproofing. Increasingly though, it is available as a mobile unit (usually called a 'rollabout') which can be moved to any room in a building. Inevitably it will become part of desktop equipment for every student and trainee. This development will take the educational model of videoconferencing away from the large lecture hall or the small group interaction towards the individual 'one learner per machine' concept. This will lead to a different form of interaction than is currently common in most educational videoconferencing.

Like audiographics, videoconferencing is a synchronous medium: same time, different place. However, what multimedia desktop conferencing will do is merge the three communications modes: text, voice and video into the same medium. By doing this, it will also make available both synchronous and asynchronous communication: text messages and video exchanges; voice annotated messages and shared screens; access to remote databases and access to the tutor. As will be shown in the individual chapters on each medium, there are educational advantages to both synchronous and asynchronous modes, as there are advantages to each of the different forms of communication: text, sound and vision. Whether multimedia desktop conferencing, which combines all these features, will amount to more than the sum of its parts, or prove to be a confusing overabundance of riches, remains to be seen.

Synchronous and asynchronous media

Although computer conferencing has been categorized as an asynchronous medium, this must be qualified. Many conferencing systems (and bulletin boards, their poor cousins) do have a synchronous 'chat' mode. This involves a shared window in which all participants can put messages. These tend to be used for socializing on an optional basis; the educational use is almost always asynchronous. The value of the medium is invariably seen to be that students and tutor can reflect on their responses and prepare a message on their machine to put into the conference at their convenience. Reading messages and considering their content – perhaps by re-reading at a later point – is also advantageous when it is at the user's instigation rather than at a set time. What happens in a computer conference which is working very successfully is that a number of messages appear in the system each day on a particular subject, such that one is continually pondering the issue. Any individual member might only make a contribution once a fortnight, but the subject is alive and developing and one is prompted to reconsider and refine one's views with each new message.

The disadvantage of asynchronous communication is that it tends, in practice, to be very prolonged. Human nature being what it is, the lack of pressure to respond immediately means that many people never get down to actually putting a message into the system. The result is what sociologists call 'communication anxiety': a student ventures forth with an opinion or point of view and no one responds for days and days (Feenberg, 1989). Those who perhaps lack self-confidence begin to feel concerned and very exposed. Others simply feel frustrated with the slow pace of interaction. Decisions amongst a group using computer conferencing – for instance, in allocating tasks for a group assignment – must wait for each member to log on and express their opinion, and perhaps even then a second round is necessary to agree on a procedure.

Synchronous communication by voice and, better still, vision overcomes the prolonging of exchanges, but of course requires immediate response. Long pauses in conversation are not acceptable and hence, 'thinking on one's feet' is necessary in synchronous communication. There are some types of learners (and teachers) who are less suited to immediate verbal responses: the reflective thinker, the student working in a second language, the academic who likes to consult references, to give a few examples. Furthermore, while synchronous meetings promote interaction in a set period of time, this event is usually ephemeral: the brilliant lecture, the engrossing discussion, the demonstration which was so simple at the time – all are inaccessible afterwards except through memory or notes.

It is obvious that there are strengths and weaknesses with both modes. What about a combination of asynchronous text messaging punctuated by synchronous events? This is what desktop conferencing promises, and a few education and training applications based on this combination are currently in their early stages. What one might call 'stitched up' versions of this combination are already familiar:

- an audiographics course with computer conferencing used for collaborative work and to access Internet resources;
- live events broadcast by satellite with fax or electronic mail (email) for questions from the audience;
- videoconferencing courses in which students submit assignments by file transfer.

Desktop conferencing will integrate the two modes on to one machine with a single interface and easy switching mechanism between the various facilities. With thorough course design and preparation, desktop conferencing offers a potentially rich environment for many types of learners.

Course delivery with telecommunications

The technologies used to transmit data, voice and video can be divided into two areas: the linking technology and user-level equipment to access the link. Link technology comprises the communications carrier (copper cable, radio or fibre-optics) and the way in which information is transmitted via that carrier (analogue or digital). The access equipment transforms signals at the user level into electronic signals for transmission. The technologies in each of these areas are in a continuous process of development. Each of the three ways of communicating (text, audio and video) involves increasing amounts of information and hence requires increasing bandwidth to transmit. The bandwidth of a communications medium is simply a measure of its capacity to carry information.

Text, in the form of messages, needs only a narrow bandwidth and can be transmitted over ordinary telephone lines using a modem to convert characters from a digital form (as held in a personal computer) into analogue form for telephone line signalling. Each text character, a letter or number, individually contains very little information and can be sent and received at relatively low speed (100 characters per second) with no effect on message content. Sound contains much more information than text and therefore takes more bandwidth. It must also be carried at the same speed as normal speech for conversation to be possible. Pictures (or still images) can require in the region of 80,000 characters to be transmitted, depending upon detail. Moving pictures, sent as a stream of several still images per second, require a very large bandwidth. If sound is included, the picture information must be sent very quickly for lip synchronization to be perceived.

The bandwidth required for full-motion colour video is over 1,500 times that of a normal telephone line. However developments in picture processing technology now make it possible to transmit such video signals in a digital form using a device called a CODEC (COder/DECoder). A CODEC at one end of a communications link transforms (or codes) analogue television signals from a video camera into a stream of digital information which is transmitted to a second CODEC at the other end of the link. This device decodes the digital information back into an analogue signal for viewing on a television monitor. The coding process compresses the picture information for more economical transmission. This involves removing any non-essential picture information and transmitting only the changes from one frame to the next. For example, a talking head against a still background only has a change in picture content of about 10 per cent from frame to frame.

Access to text-based computer conferencing systems is possible over ordinary telephones by students in their homes. Most telephone companies offer a packet-switched service which bundles data into packets for more efficient transmission to the conferencing system. This also offers lower cost access for those students who can call a local packet exchange. Higher education institutions in many countries have an academic network which students can usually use free of charge (to them). Access to the Internet, an internationally available network of connections to people and resources, is also free to users, at least currently.

Most audiographics systems running over ordinary telephone lines require one line for voice and another for the transmission of data, so home use is not realistic at the moment. When multi-site connections are used with audioconferencing, audiographics and videoconferencing, a device called a 'bridge' is necessary. This joins all the calls together into a hub for synchronous communication.

Leased lines between two locations allow the institution to pay a fixed sum for rental rather than a charge for each unit of usage of the line. Leased lines are most suited to applications requiring high levels of access such as computer-to-computer communication. Although videoconferencing can be transmitted over leased lines, the new Integrated Services Digital Network (ISDN) is much more flexible and better suited to videoconferencing patterns of usage. This is because a videoconferencing connection can be made to any other site with ISDN, whereas a leased line is fixed between two sites. ISDN requires digital public telephone switches, special adapters and conversion software at each telephone terminal. In some countries it is not available at all; in others it is available in large cities only; in a few it is available anywhere. Whether ISDN will become the standard telephone system worldwide is a contentious issue. It would certainly greatly facilitate the use of all three telecommunications technologies, but the amount of coordination and standardization necessary between all the international telephone companies makes this an unlikely dream.

Satellite is the most common carrier for international videoconferencing using either two-way digital CODEC connections or one-way broadcast television. In the latter case, ordinary telephone lines are used for an audio return for communication from the receiving sites. Conventional broadcast satellite delivery is cost-effective where there are a large number of receive sites and where the educational model is 'transmissive' (one teacher transmitting knowledge to many students). However, advances in the digital encoding of broadcast television are reducing the number of sites required for courses to be economic. For multi-way transmission between a small number of sites, VSAT technology can be more cost effective. VSATs (Very Small Aperture Terminals) can be used in a mesh system in which any site can transmit and receive.

Coaxial cable television (CATV) systems can be used to transmit video-based courses and they are connected to homes in many large cities in developed countries. However, CATV has very limited capabilities for two-way video interaction and is only cost-effective when used in one-way mode with telephone returns. Networks using a fibre-optic cable direct to the home will offer very large bandwidth communications but are very expensive to install and available only experimentally as yet.

Telecommunications and open learning

It is no coincidence that the use of telecommunications media in education and training is growing at the same time as education and training budgets are decreasing. Each of the media discussed in this book allows institutions to provide more flexible and wide-ranging access to their courses, and hence to increase student numbers without the usual increase in costs. This new openness takes various forms depending on the technology and the institutional application.

Location and time

All three technologies provide greater flexibility in the location of the educational experience than do traditional campus-based courses. Computer conferencing is often a home-based activity in which students connect to the conferencing system any time of the day or night from their own computer and telephone line. Workplace applications are also common, with employees using either a shared machine or one on their desktop, and accessing the conferencing system either in company training time or after normal work hours. Audiographics courses allow students in rural or isolated areas to take courses from a larger or more prestigious location. Students gather in a school, study centre or training room to share the communications equipment. As prices continue to fall, audiographics systems will be affordable in the home on standard computers. Of course, the timing of each session must be fixed and this is a consideration when time zones are different or when courses must fit into existing school timetables. Videoconferencing is the least flexible of the three as the necessary equipment is still very specialized. In many cases, however, students add their own flexibility by watching a recorded video of the class at home when convenient.

Curriculum

These technologies have encouraged a much wider range of course provision, in some cases on a global scale. Many computer conferencing courses offer graduate and even postgraduate degrees, and attract students from all over the world (for example, case study 1, in Chapter 7). A number of audiographics and videoconferencing courses operate transnationally (for example, the extensive training programmes of large corporations such as IBM and BP). Specialist subjects – usually in advanced technologies – are now available via telecommunications; professional updating courses in a wide variety of fields are offered with all three media; and community, leisure and adult education courses are available in more limited areas. Teleconferencing has facilitated many partnerships between prestigious institutions in developed countries and those in Eastern Europe, the Pacific Rim, Africa and South America.

In a few cases, telecommunications technologies have changed the very nature of the curriculum. The easy availability of databases, the resources of the Internet, and connection with students around the world have led to small but increasingly significant changes in the content of some courses, from primary to postgraduate level. The notion of resource-based learning – in which multimedia resources such as videos, databases, online image banks and electronic journals are made available to students and in which the teacher acts as guide and facilitator – is much more talked about than practised at present, but it takes on a new meaning with the advent of telecommunications.

The opportunities provided by technology have been beneficial not only for the learner but also for teachers and trainers. The variety of courses available is a testament to the impetus and enthusiasm telecommunications media have given to the teaching profession.

Open learning

There is much less evidence of these technologies promoting more open forms of learning. Students enrolled on most videoconferencing and audiographics courses have the same amount of class contact time, the same enrolment times and procedures, and are subject to the same regulations and prerequisites as students studying the conventional courses. Some courses delivered with computer conferencing, and to a lesser extent with audiographics, are community-based or are open to anyone with access. However, on the whole, telecommunications courses offer flexibility, not openness. The need for appropriate equipment is a further barrier to many potential students.

Gender, minorities and the disadvantaged

Whether the new telecommunications technologies have provided greater access to women, minorities and other disadvantaged learners is a subject of some debate. Early users of computer conferencing claimed that this medium positively advantaged them for the following reasons:

- the physical characteristics, gender and disability of the learner are not apparent to other users;
- those using their second language have time to prepare messages carefully and read messages slowly;
- any number of users can contribute their ideas, not just the loquacious students.

Many articles in the computer conferencing literature give testimony to the advantages of this medium for various minorities and types of disabled students. When the problem of access to suitable equipment is solved, women seem to take a more equal part in online discussions than in comparable face-to-face situations.

The relative anonymity and home-based nature of computer conferencing make it much more supportive of gender equality and minority and disabled access than either of the synchronous technologies. Audiographics has a similar focus on the content rather than the person, but does require immediate rather than delayed responses. However, audioconferencing with students using their home telephone is probably the most advantageous to minorities and the disabled, and requires much less equipment than computer conferencing.

Quality

Distance education has, until very recently, been considered the poor cousin of traditional face-to-face education or training. This attitude is gradually changing in the wake of experience, telecommunications and new educational challenges.

Many studies have been carried out which compare traditional courses with those delivered by telecommunications. American research almost invariably looks at final grades as the determinant of comparability. Even this very crude indicator almost always shows no difference in outcomes, and in fact often shows slightly better results from students learning via one of these three media.

Qualitative evaluation reports on many courses using these media note that students felt they had more contact, more stimulation and a more rewarding educational experience than with comparable face-to-face taught courses (for example, Blantern and Press, 1993; Souder, 1993). One explanation for these comments might well be that any innovation requires extra energy and attention from the teacher. Furthermore, many of these courses attract the most committed and enthusiastic teachers. Once telecommunications technologies become the rule rather than the exception – and predictions to this effect are common – the quality of courses using these media will probably reflect the standard of teaching generally. Be that as it may, many teachers have, through these media, found a new enthusiasm for their subject and a pleasure in participating with students in its unfolding. Quality of educational provision lies ultimately in that pleasure.

Telecommunications and distance education

The term 'distance education' – what it means and what educational provisions it encompasses – is fast becoming an historical debate. Place-based education and distance education have been on converging paths for some time. Telecommunications have brought about their collision! So many teaching and training institutions now use telecommunications media to augment, extend and enhance face-to-face meetings, and so many students at one institution take courses from another, that the concept of distance is no longer the real issue.

For example, computer conferencing is used as much at campus-based institutions as it is with home-based students (for an example, see Hosley,

1987). On campus, it is used to:

- offer greater time flexibility to students, (they can come in to use terminals at their convenience to access parts of a course, or perhaps to take an entire course online);
- provide better opportunities for interaction with the lecturer, or to practise writing or second-language skills with peers;
- make connections with students around the world via the Internet.

These students probably live locally, but may have jobs or family commitments which make full-time class attendance undesirable or impossible. In any case, computer conferencing provides opportunities which face-to-face teaching does not (for example, Hoffman, 1993). The same is true for some applications of videoconferencing, although for different reasons.

Distance education used to conjure up an image of an isolated student working with printed material and relying on the postal system for any interaction with the teacher. As Chapter 2 will make clear, telecommunications technologies have increased communications, in some cases to a greater extent than in face-to-face teaching.

Audiographics and videoconferencing clearly have students at a distance, but when students at one institution connect with students and a teacher at another, the term 'distance education' no longer seems appropriate. In any case, with some applications, the teacher takes it in turn to initiate the session from alternate sites. In many training situations, a tutor is available at each site to coordinate the course and to facilitate discussion after the live session.

The fact that the term 'distance education' has become very blurred does not mean that there are no longer differences between face-to-face and telecommunications-based courses. This book is about the distinct properties of the latter, and Chapter 3 looks specifically at the implications of these differences for students, teachers and organizations.

Summary

This chapter has laid a foundation for looking at three technologies currently used in education and training: computer conferencing, audiographics and videoconferencing. Their significance in relation to open and flexible learning has been discussed, and their role in displacing traditional views of distance education has been noted.

The convergence of these three media into multimedia desktop conferencing, with its attendant possibilities for resource-based learning, has been raised as a vision (or perhaps a spectre to some) to bear in mind during the more detailed chapters which follow.

References

Blantern, C and Press, D (1993) 'Self development through interactive writing', in Mason, R (ed.) *Computer Conferencing: The last word*, British Columbia: Beach Holme Publishers.

Feenberg, A (1989) 'The written word', in Mason, R and Kaye, A R (eds) *Mindweave: Communication, computers and distance education*, Oxford: Pergamon.

Hoffman, R (1993) 'The distance brings us closer: electronic mail, ESL learner writers and teachers', in Davies, G and Samways, B (eds) *Teleteaching*, Proceedings of the IFIP TC3 Third Teleteaching Conference, Trondheim, Norway, Amsterdam: North-Holland.

Hosley, C (1987) 'How to get reaction from students in big, impersonal lecture classes', *Chronicle of Higher Education*, **33**, 34.

Souder, W (1993) 'The effectiveness of traditional versus satellite delivery in three management of technology master's degree programs', *The American Journal of Distance Education*, **7**, 1, 37–52.

Chapter 2

Interaction

What is it?

No concept so characterizes educational thinking in the 1990s as does interactivity. It is intertwined with the growth of several other areas of educational concern: open and distance learning, student-centred learning and holistic education. So embedded in the spirit of the age is it that there is relatively little questioning of its value, much less evaluation of its effects. Teachers are said to require it in order to know whether they are communicating effectively; students are supposed to need it to clarify any misunderstandings; distance education is thought to be enlivened and de-packaged by interaction. What is meant by the term and why is it considered such a good thing?

The word 'interactivity' is currently used in a wide variety of ways. The obvious meaning – communication between two or more people – is by no means the only one. Computer-based training and interactive video are frequently referred to as interactive: students can stop and start when they choose, can go at their own pace, are offered choices which may lead in different directions; sometimes they can choose different routes through the material. Even print material, when written as a conversation in a personal style with in-text questions and model answers, is considered interactive.

The term is also used rather indiscriminately in relation to purpose and quality. For instance, systems which allow voting or polling have a different value educationally from a system used for small group discussion, although both are called 'interactive'. Much of what passes for interactivity should really be called 'feedback' – to the organization or the teacher. It would be useful if the word 'interactivity' were reserved for educational situations in which human responses – either vocal or written – referred to previous human responses. The educational value of any specific interactive session could then be seen in terms of the degree to which each utterance built on previous ones.

Despite the lack of clarity on this issue and the relative lack of evaluation of its technology-mediated applications, there is much theoretical support for its importance (Armstrong, 1990; Rafaeli, 1988; Tucker, 1989). Communication is a strong human need and closely involved with learning. Interaction has been shown to benefit learners at the affective level. It increases motivation and interest in the subject. In training contexts, interactivity has been shown to increase the speed of assimilation and length and degree of retention of information. Opportunities for learners to express their own points of view, explain the issues in their own words and to formulate opposing or different arguments, have always been related to deep-level learning and the development of critical thinking.

> Most theories of learning suggest that for learning to be effective it needs to be active; in other words the learner must respond in some way to the learning material. It is not enough merely to observe or read; learners have to do something with the learning material. Thus they may need to demonstrate (if only to themselves) that they have understood, or they may need to reprocess new material to incorporate it with existing knowledge, or to apply the new knowledge they have acquired successfully to new situations (Bates, 1991)

Seen in this light, it is not surprising that interactivity is regarded as a positive benefit to education and training. The much-derided passivity of television and the isolating effects of correspondence education have only increased the credentials of interaction as a *sine qua non* of the best programmes. This seems to have created a bandwagon effect such that every programme, every technology, every approach is labelled 'interactive' – by some obscure definition of the word.

Interactive technologies

Technology-mediated courses have a related 'image problem'. Because traditional face-to-face teaching continues to be the model which all other teaching seeks to imitate, technologies are generally rated by the degree to which they reproduce the classroom scenario. Despite this, evaluators and researchers of technology-based courses continually conclude that they will be really successful when the particular technology is exploited for its unique facilities, not for its verisimilitude to traditional teaching. Chapters 4, 5 and 6 will look at what is unique in each of the three media discussed in this book. In terms of interactivity, it is interesting to look at how students of technology-mediated courses react to the opportunity for interaction.

In considering interactivity on computer conferencing, audiographics and videoconferencing courses, it is necessary to bear in mind the nature of interaction in most face-to-face teaching situations. Studies of classroom interaction have produced the well-known 'initiation, response, feedback' pattern: the teacher asks a question, a student responds and the teacher evaluates the response. The ratio of teacher to student dialogue may easily be as high as 80:20. By the time most students reach tertiary education or professional training, they have experienced roughly 13 years of this very limited type of interaction. Although many adult learners are much more active and questioning in their learning than they were as children, there remains a legacy of passivity and teacher-led models of the learning experience which are difficult to overcome.

Statistics on the frequency of interaction vary with the nature of the technology application. Small learning groups using any of the three media of concern here show much higher levels and quality of interaction than large groups using the same technology. So obviously interactivity is not a characteristic of the medium, but of its particular application. The UK Open University's pioneering use of computer conferencing with 1,500 undergraduates has consistently each year had about one third of the students using the system actively to put in messages; about one third reading messages regularly and one third taking little or no part in its use. The low take-up of the interactive capability of videoconferencing is one of its best-kept secrets – when figures are given, they are frequently lower than the course designers expected. Students are delighted when one of their peers asks a question or makes a point they had in mind, but many are too intimidated to do this themselves. In fact, many of the live videoconferencing courses offered throughout North America are actually taped and watched later, at the students' convenience, as this provides the needed flexibility for adult learners. There are other studies which support the view that students do not rate interactivity as highly as often assumed (Stone, 1990). Comparing the facility to ask questions after a video lecture with other forms of student support, such as feedback on assignments, access to library facilities, telephone office hours with the lecturer, students did not put live video interactivity near the top of the list (Barnard, 1992). Some studies even report that students find interactivity a waste of teaching time and some (undergraduate) students of a computer conferencing course always skipped messages by their peers and only read their teacher's messages.

A number of studies also report that there is little or no difference in final results between students who have the potential for interactivity (for example, two-way videoconferencing or face-to-face teaching) and those who do not (for example, one-way video). In fact, some educators are beginning to question the value of two-way videoconferencing, given its much higher cost and infrastructure, the relative lack of use of the interactive capability and the research findings that the interactivity does not improve students' final marks (Russell, 1993).

Although the quantity and quality of interaction using audiographics systems is generally much higher – due to the much smaller size of learning groups – the interactive capability of the shared whiteboard is often underused in many applications. In fact, the drawing or text on the screen often acts as a focusing device, like an overhead slide in a face-to-face lecture, to follow the voice communication. Useful as this may be, it is not interactive. Considerable planning and preparation on the part of the teacher is usually necessary for a successful audiographics session in which students interact both orally and graphically.

Does this mean that students would really be happy with non-interactive courses? The answer is no, but the reasons are complex. Open University students, asked why they liked computer conferencing so much when they hadn't used it interactively, said they felt much less isolated knowing they could use it if they needed, and students of videoconferencing courses value the questions asked by their peers, even though they may watch by video at a later point. Undoubtedly the confident student who uses the opportunity to communicate with teacher and peers gains tremendously from the facility. Many enthusiastic student responses attest to the positive benefits of interactive teaching media. The importance to students of the psychological support from knowing that interactivity is possible, should not be underestimated. Evaluation studies also show that students of computer conferencing courses who participate largely by reading the messages of others are positive about their gains from interactive courses. Teachers of videoconferencing courses consistently comment on the importance of seeing and getting feedback from their remote students.

Studies of courses using any of these three media tend to show that when students perceive interaction to be high, they have a more positive sense of satisfaction with the course. However, students' perception of the amount of interaction that occurs on the same course varies considerably (see, for example, Fulford and Zhang, 1993, who conducted a study comparing students' perception with actual levels of interaction as recorded on video tapes).

Interactivity on demand?

The issue which is often debated by teachers who regularly use these media is: should students be encouraged or even forced to participate? Should teachers put distant students on the spot by inviting them by name to answer a question? Should computer conferencing students be marked on the quality of their contributions to the conference? Opinions vary as to whether these methods operate against an educational experience which is fun, invariably positive and comfortable, or whether they help to sustain interest and attention. The answer to these questions depends completely on context: the learning situation, the nature of the students and the way in which the teacher interacts with students. What would intimidate in one context would create a lively learning atmosphere in another. For example, students on one Open University course said they wanted to be marked on their contributions as an indication of the value and importance of this element of the course. When an online assigment was introduced, students did respond positively: much higher usage rates during the assignment period and real interactivity of messaging. On another course, however, students rebelled against the idea of marks for contributions, saying it would destroy the spontaneous and interactive nature of the discussion and turn it into a scoring club. In videoconferencing sessions, it has been shown that if the interaction excludes one site, students at that site pay less attention. Facilitating communication between learners at different sites is thought to be a useful approach for presenters.

In small group work using audiographics, interactivity is at the very heart of the teaching. Cooperative work, either joint presentations, group projects or small group discussions, usually forms a large element of the course. Sometimes this collaboration is deliberately set across sites in order to expose students to the ideas of their peers at other institutions; sometimes it is devised so that the inter-site activity is suspended for a period during a session and students can discuss issues or prepare a response by working in face-to-face self-help groups on their own. Audiographics manuals for teachers usually recommend that students be called by name to answer questions or respond to particular issues.

Keeping interaction alive is much like throwing a ball around the room; no one is sure to whom it will come or who will catch it. Everyone's mind is attentive even if they don't catch or throw the ball. The game itself keeps everyone interested (Fulford and Zhang, 1993, p. 260).

Although videoconferencing can be used for collaborative work (see case study 7, in Chapter 7), this usage is not the most common. Videoconferencing tends to be used in situations which replicate face-to-face lecturing – not a teaching method known for deep-level human interactivity, let alone collaborative work. As financial pressures on tertiary education increase, the need to teach more students with fewer resources seems unlikely to create an environment for increasing small group seminars. In terms of its most common application, videoconferencing more or less perpetuates the interactivity level and quality pertaining in face-to-face lectures. This will vary from teacher to teacher depending on their personal style and approach to teaching. Questions from students and answers from the teacher typify most current applications. Students may be slightly more intimidated by the presence of cameras in initiating questions 'at a distance', but a good presenter can easily overcome this with a relaxed, approachable manner.

The interactive medium most often used in print-based distance education is computer conferencing. Here the technology provides a new opportunity for interactivity which was only possible through postal communication before. As Chapter 4 will show, this has the potential to transform distance education from 'second best' after face-to-face education to a first rate educational environment with flexibility and student-centred interactivity.

The most advanced distance education programs can provide students with far greater involvement in the process of learning and allow them the exercise of far greater control over that process than is possible in many traditional learning environments. ... Substantial teacher/student interaction, for many years a perceived weakness of distance education programs, is rapidly becoming an asset of the method while it grows as a liability in many of our traditional classrooms (Task Force Report, 1993).

This extract highlights one of the most enduring myths about interactivity: that face-to-face education is a hotbed of intellectual discussion both in and out of class. With increasing pressure of student numbers at most tertiary institutions, the amount of teacher/student interactivity is now actually very small. Ironically, in fact, telecommunications courses may come to be the leader in interactivity in education and training.

Collaborative work

The increasing amount of team work in business and industry has encouraged educators and trainers to develop more collaborative learning practices in their courses. Interactive technologies now support these practices at a distance, and this has in turn increased interest in developing collaborative projects, discussions and presentations in adult education and training. Figure 2.1 shows videoconferencing facilitating group work.

Another aspect to the growing interest in collaborative work is the move away from transmissive models of teaching in which authority and knowledge are vested in the teacher and the student assumes a relatively passive role. Instead, the constructivist model is based on a theory of

Photo courtesy of PictureTel

Figure 2.1 *Collaborative work through videoconferencing*

learning in which meaning is derived from and embedded in context. It therefore places more emphasis on group activity in the learning process, peer exchange and social networking, and enhances rather than devalues the contextual and social factors of the learning environment.

> This movement is accompanied, of necessity, by changes in the traditional roles of both learners and tutors: learners are expected to take a more active and constructive role, contributing from their own experience and knowledge as appropriate; tutors are expected to be facilitators and resource people, as well as course planners and knowledge brokers (Kaye, 1993).

Computer conferencing is a collaborative medium par excellence – but primarily for discussion, brainstorming, role playing and joint presentations. One type of collaboration which it is notoriously unsuccessful at supporting is any kind of group decision making. For example, when a number of students are given a task which they must divide up amongst themselves, they can spend most of their time simply negotiating who will do what. An asynchronous medium does not encourage closure or coming to decisions, unless a natural leader emerges. However, if pairs or small groups are asked to prepare a presentation on a particular issue or reading, they can form their own topic on the system, discuss different opinions and then make a report in the conference for the whole group. Another possibility is for the tutor to simply designate one student as leader of a small group, and this can lessen the asynchronous problems of collaborative work. Other kinds of successful collaborations involve students contributing comments and ideas to a set question, debating an issue in pairs, or conducting a mock investigation with different role-playing parts.

With audiographics, the natural grouping is usually those students sharing one set of equipment. However, it is often desirable to make groupings across sites, in order to make cross-cultural liaisons or to work with peers from different settings or contexts. In either case, collaborative work is almost always an integral part of audiographics teaching. As sessions tend to last at least an hour, it is possible and indeed desirable to break up the time with a variety of activities. Often the telecommunications link is broken for part of the time so that small group discussions can take place. Cross-site interactions sometimes take place without the teacher, during which time students can prepare their presentation for the whole group.

Collaborative work in small group videoconferences is much the same as with audiographics – verbal discussions and shared drawings or other graphics. Collaborative work and large videoconferencing lectures are virtually incompatible, although an inventive lecturer might ask students to discuss an issue with the person sitting beside them for five minutes as a change of pace.

One of the most important outcomes of collaborative work is that it helps students take more responsibility for their own learning. The teacher is no longer centre-stage; the learners have to navigate their way through information and ideas, solve problems together and, finally, present their results in an ordered and persuasive way.

Assessment of collaboratively produced work is a difficult issue, whether telecommunications are involved or not. Various strategies have been used, depending on the teaching objectives:

- some part of the mark for individual effort and some part for the group effort;
- one mark applicable to all participants regardless of their individual input
- some form of negotiated mark, in which either the individual or the group decides, in consultation with the tutor, what individual mark each participant deserves.

Social presence

One of the issues currently debated amongst designers of interactive software for collaborative work is how to create a sense of social presence. What contributes to the feeling that the people with whom you are collaborating are right there in the room with you? Icons showing the faces of each person in a small group working together are one example of a software solution to heightening social presence for online collaboration sessions.

Each of the three interactive technologies described here has a different way of enhancing social presence. At first guess, computer conferencing might be thought to be the least successful in creating a sense of the presence of others. It has the most limited bandwidth – text only – and is asynchronous, so in fact other people are not present either in location or in time. Indeed, some who try computer conferencing once or twice and do not like it, tend to complain about the lack of social presence: 'I didn't know anyone to communicate with'; 'You've got to be able to talk with other people; writing is too slow'. These are typical responses from those who do not relate to the kind of social presence computer conferencing offers. However, there is much evidence from those who do enjoy the medium that computer conferencing interaction is often more personal, more intimate and more community-creating than comparable face-to-face situations:

> 'This medium not only made communication possible, it made it unexpectedly deeper.'

> 'Answering your electronic questions is more like engaging in a personal conversation with you than it is formal writing.'

> 'I am moved by your thoughts and feelings. It's almost as if a wave of emotion came out of the monitor towards me.'

Computer conferencing supports a kind of intimacy which is one element of the feeling of social presence.

Audiographics, like audioconferencing, is dependent on the voice to create a sense of presence. However, when many different voices come one after the other, it is often hard to distinguish who is speaking. This is by far the most disconcerting aspect of voice media. In multi-site audiographics sessions, each site is sometimes assigned one colour from the graphics palette, so that everyone knows who is drawing. In audioconferencing, everyone is usually asked to identify themselves each time they speak. Needless to say, this contributes to an awkward, formal atmosphere, and is dropped as soon as voice recognition is developed.

Many videoconferencing sales brochures advertise their products with slogans such as, 'better than being there' or more modestly, 'as good as being there'. Certainly the visual presence of others does enhance a strong sense of social presence. When videoconferencing is used in small group situations, it is very successful at creating a social environment for learning. When it is used for large lectures, as is often the case, some educators question the value of the visual image of the lecturer. In strictly cognitive terms, the visual presence of the lecturer adds little. Merely seeing the lecturer is a waste of expensive bandwidth, the argument goes. However, those who believe that social presence makes a significant contribution to the learning environment dispute the content-focus of their detractors. Nothing can give the remote student the feeling of participating in a live event so satisfactorily as videoconferencing.

As has been underlined many times, it is not the technology but the way it is used, which ultimately affects the learner. A good teacher has presence in any medium.

Conclusions

Interactivity in educational terms has three dimensions:

- interaction between the student and the content – whether in text, a computer program, video material or multimedia combinations;
- interaction between the teacher and the student – whether in question and answer sessions after lectures, by telephone, fax or email, in office hours or in class;
- interaction between students – whether in self-help groups, collaborative work projects, or in discussions and seminars.

Telecommunications technologies facilitate the latter two forms particularly. However, the quality of the interaction, whether it reinforces factual transmission of information, or develops critical thinking and team-working skills, is a result of the course design and outlook of the teacher.

Interactivity at a price

The next chapter looks at the implications of the use of these technologies for teachers, learners and institutions. Making interactive technologies available does not lead inevitably to good interaction. Collaborative practices are very new to many teachers, and they require time and energy to develop. Even when teachers are keen to experiment, they may well run up against institutional barriers. First of all, interactivity and large student numbers are not easily compatible. Administrators look to telecommunications strategies to increase numbers and reduce costs. Adding online tutors to engage students interactively or hiring site facilitators at distant locations, are two solutions to large numbers, but both increase costs.

Finally, students often present the biggest hurdle of all. As indicated earlier, many students are reluctant to initiate questions, engage in interaction or work independently of the teacher. This holds true in traditional face-to-face teaching, but even more so, at a distance. Undoubtedly this is partly because it is hard work! Teachers sometimes need perseverence to convince students that collaborative interaction is a vital part of learning.

References

Armstrong, B (1990) 'STARNET: Interactive training by satellite', *Educational and Training Technology International*, **27**, 3, 249–53.

Barnard, J (1992) 'Video-based instruction: issues of effectiveness, interaction, and learner control', *Journal of Educational Technology Systems*, **21**, 1, 45–50.

Bates, A W (1991) 'Interactivity as a criterion for media selection in distance education', *Never Too Far*, **16**, 5–9.

Fulford, C and Zhang, S (1993) 'Predicting student satisfaction from perceptions of interaction in distance learning', in Davies, G and Samways B (eds), *Teleteaching*, Proceedings of the IFIP TC3 Third Teleteaching Conference, Trondheim, Norway, Amsterdam: North-Holland.

Kaye, A (1993) 'Co-learn: A multimedia environment for collaborative learning', in Mason, R and Bacsich, P (eds.) *ISDN Applications in Education and Training*, Institution of Electrical Engineers: London.

Rafaeli, S (1988) 'Interactivity: From new media to communication', in Hawkins, R, Weimann, J and Pingree, S (eds) *Advancing Communication Science: Merging Mass and Interpersonal Processes*, Newbury Park, CA: Sage.

Russell, T (1993) 'A medium revisited: televised distance education', in Davies, G and Samways, B (eds) *Teleteaching*, Proceedings of the IFIP TC3 Third Teleteaching Conference, Trondheim, Norway, Amsterdam: North-Holland.

Stone, H (1990) 'Does interactivity matter in video-based off-campus graduate engineering education?', College Industry Education Conference Proceedings, 17–27.

Task Force Report (1993) Pennsylvania State University, November 1992, *DEOSNEWS*, **3**, 7.

Tucker, R (ed.) (1989) *Interactive Media: The human issues*, London: Kogan Page.

Chapter 3

Implications for students, teachers and organizations

> In general, conferencing technologies should be tools to help human activities. But like models of teaching, they are not neutral tools. Their use will reflect whatever values the educator holds – consciously or subconsciously – about her/his relationship with learners, and their use will invariably bring advantages and disadvantages (Burge and Roberts, 1993, p. 35).

The context in which any of these three conferencing technologies is used reflects attitudes to education on the part of the organization and the particular teacher. This context defines the advantages and disadvantages for all concerned. Small group discussion is a different learning situation altogether from a large lecture. A print-based course with an occasional audiographics session is quite different from an audiographics course with a printed study guide.

Interaction is all very well, but how is the content of the course to be delivered? In postgraduate and professional updating courses, the exchange of ideas and experience may be paramount. For many other contexts, however, the conveying of a body of knowledge is a prime objective of the course. Print materials, either written specially for the course, or in the form of set texts or articles, are the most usual accompaniment to computer conferencing and audiographics courses. Lecturing is the most common method with videoconferencing.

What these three technologies have in common is that students are not in the same location as the teacher and/or other students, at least not during use of the medium. This fact has a number of implications – for equipment provision, learning styles, preparation of teaching material, and not least, training and support.

Implications for students

Most evaluation studies on educational uses of conferencing include feedback from students regarding their reactions to learning from the medium. Almost invariably reports are enthusiastic. Students are usually positive about the advantages the medium has brought them: a wider curriculum choice, less time and money spent travelling, more interactivity with the teacher and their peers. Where reports are less favourable are quasi-laboratory studies in which students are put into both remote classrooms and face-to-face teaching situations and the results of tests compared. The fact is that with a few exceptions, these systems are used to meet specific needs: time, distance, interaction, etc. When these systems are used outside of any context of need, the results, not surprisingly, show less user acceptance.

How well do these systems meet students' needs? The travel time and distance needs are best met by home-based technologies, or workplace settings. Audiographics tends to be used in study centres, which can be very convivial settings with a long cultural tradition. The social and interactive needs of students vary considerably: some students prefer to learn in isolation; others want some contact with their peers. Face-to-face contact is the only satisfactory form of interaction for some students; others find the curiously intimate but anonymous quality of computer conferencing contact very appealing. Undoubtedly videoconferencing is most satisfactory to most students in meeting social and interactive learning needs. On the whole, the greater the need and motivation for access to education and training, the more these technologies are perceived by students as satisfactory.

The question of transferring costs to students arises with home-based computer conferencing – the initial purchase of computer equipment and the ongoing cost of telephone calls. Training, maintenance and upgrading of the equipment are additional problems with costs attached. In many parts of the world, however, a computer in the home is inappropriate; it requires too much personal space and needs to be connected to a telephone line nearby. For example, even in the UK, one Open University study concluded that for remote students, print, audio cassettes and the telephone were still the most viable distance technologies (Deacon, 1993).

Innumerable studies have shown that students' marks on final examinations are not determined by the medium. The quality of the teaching is a much more significant determinant. What is significant in relation to the media is the long-term appeal they evoke in learners. Any innovation has a short-term positive effect – in these cases due to the extra attention teachers and organizations put into launching the innovation.

Videoconferencing has been used educationally for over ten years and can only be said to be growing in acceptance. As this medium is most often used in traditional lecture format, the obvious conclusion is that the majority of students are not questioning this form of teaching, and notice little change whether the lecture is delivered face-to-face or by video.

This conclusion is confirmed by the long-term users of computer conferencing, the medium which most challenges the traditional lecture format. In fact, computer conferencing requires much more self-direction, motivation and initiative on the part of the student than do most other media. Although applications in this area are also growing very fast, the overall student acceptance level is probably lowest. Computer conferencing is hard work for students, much more so than listening to a lecture. There are not many precedents for interactive discussion in education – discussions in which one is expected to formulate a point of view, express it and modify or defend it in the face of comment or criticism. Many teachers cannot or choose not to use interactive teaching methods. Any experience students have had in doing this is almost invariably spoken rather than written. Although many students are very enthusiastic about computer conferencing, there is no doubt that many others are not. Most tutors report that their main difficulty lies in encouraging students to participate.

As the case studies in Chapter 7 show, some students are very nervous about making presentations via videoconferencing. Having to manage equipment and being seen on monitors simply add to the general level of stress in presenting their own work. Audiographics presentations seem to cause less concern, presumably because there is no camera to record embarrassment and nervousness.

The impact of these technologies on students varies with how active and interactive they choose to be. Students who want to take the initiative in the learning process and who enjoy engaging with their peers are empowered by these technologies. Others will use them to learn this independence and interdependence. Nevertheless, there will always remain a minority resistant to these technologies, for whom face-to-face is the only satisfactory learning mode.

Training and support for students

If videoconferencing is used in lecture mode, students need no training in using the equipment, but in more interactive uses of the medium, students do need to learn how to operate the equipment. A practice session for this and for audiographics is recommended before the official start of the course, in which students get to know each other and the equipment.

With computer conferencing, training is usually more problematic, yet more necessary. Learning to use a conferencing system has three elements: logging onto the system, navigating around the various areas, and becoming an active and interactive user. The first of these is peculiar to the individual student's equipment, telephone line and location. Procedures learned at a training session may not work when applied at home. A telephone help desk to handle queries about equipment and communications is a valuable support for students. Learning the commands and structure of a

Photo courtesy of VIS-A-VIS

Figure 3.1 *An audiographics class*

conferencing system can be done from a manual or by trial and error. An offline demonstration program is occasionally provided to students for this purpose. The third element in the process is the most difficult to teach – how to become an active learner, at least within the context of computer conferencing. It requires a combination of practice and good teaching.

The question of whether a face-to-face meeting is necessary or just desirable in this process is often debated. Most teachers recommend at least one face-to-face meeting in order to establish a group feeling, and when this happens at the beginning of the course, it is usually combined with training. In many situations, however, it is simply impossible to bring people together or to offer hands-on training. Obviously it is more difficult to develop easy group relations and, in the case of computer conferencing, more difficult to develop interactive use.

Figure 3.1 shows a small, remote audiographics class in which no local facilitator is present. Larger classes or sites which are in a different country from the host site would usually require some support person. This applies to videoconferencing as well.

Implications for teachers

Preparation

Whereas computer conferencing demands most from students, audio-graphics and videoconferencing demand most from teachers. Without exception, reports about these two media indicate that preparation time is much greater than for equivalent face-to-face teaching. This preparation is of two sorts: producing visual material and planning the format of the session. The more interaction desired, the more planning is necessary.

The quality of the visuals used is a significant element in the success of these media. The size and legibility of the lettering and drawings, the production of graphics or other images, require that the teacher be competent in the use of graphics software or have access to a support team. Sequencing the images to be used requires planning at the 'story-board' level of detail – what course concepts will be conveyed with each image and how to make one flow into the next to create a meaningful narrative. The use of video clips, whether pre-existing or made in-house, requires even more preparation with videoconferencing. Devising collaborative activities for students is another consideration, as well as planning how to facilitate interactive discussion. One set of guidelines suggests:

Questions to learners participating at distant sites should be preplanned and range from low-order (recall of knowledge) to higher-order (synthesis, analysis, problem solving etc.) on Bloom's taxonomy of cognitive questions. The teleteacher needs to ask a lot of questions in order to 'force' interaction with the learners. After posing a question, the teacher should allow sufficient 'wait' time for students to process information before they answer (Barker and Goodwin, 1992).

With videoconferencing, teachers need to project themselves, rather like actors, and create a dynamic presence to convey their subject over a monitor. Audiographics instructors need to develop their listening skills in order to coordinate interaction from several sites.

The role of the computer conferencing teacher is the farthest removed from that of the traditional lecturer. Course design is equally as important as with the other technologies, and preparation entails the structuring of conferences and topics and the design of activities and small group work. During the course, however, the teacher's role is definitely one of facilitator and host, rather than one of content provider and star of the show.

The facilitator needs to pay careful attention to welcoming each student to the electronic course, and reinforcing early attempts to communicate. In the first few weeks, I make sure that my notes in the conference specifically reference prior student notes. I send many individual messages to students commenting on their contribution, suggesting links to other students, suggesting resources, and generally reaching out to students. The coaching function is key to easing the students' transition to computer-mediated communication (Davie, 1989, p. 82).

While the teacher's role is particularly time-consuming in the initial phase of a computer conferencing course, it usually reduces as students take over the discussions. Nevertheless, some reports indicate that teachers spend up to twice as long, overall, to give a course via computer conferencing as they do to give a course by traditional means.

Rewards

Most teachers who take on the challenge of teleconferencing, particularly those who develop collaborative learning strategies for their courses, report tremendous satisfaction despite the greater effort required. The reward lies in their sense of working towards the goal of developing independent, questioning learners. Almost all find that using these technologies is a tremendous learning experience for themselves:

> These experiences also taught me how to teach differently than in a traditional classroom. They have led me to reflect on my role as a teacher, and have enabled me to change my teaching style to facilitate learner-centred instructional systems that promote knowledge generation through collaborative learning. The quality of student interactions and performance has shown that students were able to generate knowledge, to innovate, to collaborate, and to analyze their own learning. The teacher's role in interactive telecommunication teaching is best portrayed as that of a facilitator guiding and supporting the learning process. This is no easy task, and consumes much more time and energy than does teaching a traditional class. The role changes I have experienced as a result of distance teaching have been transferred to my traditional teaching in that my teaching style has become learner centered and interactive (Gunawardena, 1982).

One of the additional rewards for computer conferencing teachers lies in the flexibility it gives them to work at their convenience, not at set times.

Training and support for teachers

With all three of these technologies, training and support for the teacher are critical. Most institutions develop written material for teachers, but hands-on training is also necessary. Familiarity with the equipment is fundamental for developing confidence in teaching with it. A videotaped teaching session for the new teacher, followed by a review and discussion of weak points, is ideal for videoconferencing. For audiographics, practice in using the equipment is usually adequate, but observing a multi-site class in action also helps to understand the dynamics of the situation. Computer conferencing requires a certain degree of familiarity with the system commands and architecture, but most teachers express a wish for more training in how to moderate conferences – promoting discussion, devising activities and encouraging interaction. This is a much more difficult skill and although experienced online teachers have written guidelines, in the end teachers must find their own style through practice.

Support for teachers using teleconferencing varies with the technology, and as it invariably represents an ongoing cost, only the largest or best financed programmes usually provide it. In fact, the capability of a technology to be operated by the teacher single-handedly is necessary in many contexts. With computer conferencing, a technical assistant to answer students' queries about their equipment or their connections is particularly welcome, as most teachers do not have that expertise, and in any case, handling these queries can be very time-consuming. With audiographics, a facilitator at each site, who sets up the equipment, perhaps coordinates small group discussion during or after the session, and carries out other administrative duties, is used in some applications. Help in preparing graphics and other visual material is another form of support with both this and videoconferencing. Technical assistants during videoconferencing lectures operate camera switching and manage the visuals with some systems; with others, the teachers manage these things themselves.

Implications for organizations

Introduction of telecommunications

The context in which teleconferencing technologies are introduced in an organization involves many institutional policy issues. For example, the fee structure for 'distance' courses needs to be considered: are telecommunications costs to be included and is the programme expected to save money? The increase in consortia of educational institutions offering telecommunications courses brings up the question of accreditation and approval of the curriculum. Assessment strategies also need to be re-thought with students learning at a distance.

If the programme involves teachers in major changes, it is essential to plan and market the innovation very carefully. Most telecommunications applications have been championed originally by one or two members of an organization. Wider acceptance and use of the medium depend on whether teachers are involved and consulted in the process.

Support

A number of case studies and evaluations of telecommunications applications underline the importance of top-level administrative support to the success of any programme. Although many small-scale uses of these technologies begin at grass-roots level with a few enthusiastic teachers, their growth within an organization must have backing at the highest levels because so many major policy issues are at stake.

The provision of support for students is a major issue an organization must address. The quality of these support services is equally as important to student motivation and performance as are the teleconferences. These usually involve some print material: accompanying notes with student exercises, supporting documents, and especially a study guide. The organization must consider the preparation and delivery of these to students. Many institutions offer their distance students telephone office hours for direct queries with their teacher. Individualized feedback from faculty on assessments and access to library resources (increasingly via electronic communications) are other forms of support. Operating a help desk for queries about equipment and communications systems is another institutional consideration for those involved in computer conferencing. Given the technical complications of the current telecommunications scene, many organizations adopt the policy of expecting students to turn to their local dealer for this support.

Managing and supporting the equipment through its lifetime is another issue which some institutions face for the first time with telecommunications. For some organizations, a whole new unit and type of staff are necessary. Many underestimate the extent of this element of telecommunications:

> To understate the dollars required to operate, maintain, upgrade, and train to the system is to undercut its assimilation into the instructional process. When this happens, technology remains supplemental, making it even more vulnerable to cost reductions (Maloy and Perry, 1991).

Incentives for faculty

Support for teachers takes the form of providing technical back-up or assistance in the preparation of printed, graphic or video material. However, a more significant organizational policy issue is the question of incentives and remuneration of faculty who teach via telecommunications. Despite the extra workload involved in all three of these technologies, very few institutions currently acknowledge these efforts of their teaching staff with additional payment. Furthermore, the tertiary education promotion process does not adequately reward faculty for taking on teleconferencing duties. Long-term users of these systems state this lack of recognition as a significant deterrent to growth and acceptance amongst faculty.

This issue is bound up with the much more complex and long-term issue of whether these technologies save money.

Cost savings

Cost studies of actual uses of these technologies are very rare (exceptions include Rawlings *et al.*, 1993 and Rumble, 1989). Generalizations from the few which exist are notoriously difficult to apply to other contexts. Most articles concerning training applications claim that cost savings are one of the major justifications for their introduction (see, for example, Lange, 1993). Other studies conclude that telecommunications systems do not save money in the long run. What they do is extend access to courses, improve the quality of current provision and meet needs which cannot otherwise be accommodated.

Another consideration is the cost-benefit of the secondary uses of telecommunications facilities. These include staff development, administration, and community outreach. Most applications involve some or all of these secondary uses and, in a few cases, they have come to be valued more than the primary intended uses.

The question of whether to buy equipment or lease space on commercially available systems is one that organizations should weigh up very carefully. In fact, very few do. The cost of buying equipment can be easily assessed, and relatively easily passed through finance departments. The much greater costs of support tend to get overlooked or buried in other budgets, and programmes suffer. Leasing is an option which often is not even considered, yet it can provide an interim solution for organizations which have no expertise in telecommunications. As this expertise builds up through experience, the organization is better placed to consider which equipment and systems to buy for their particular context. Meantime, support and even training can be carried out by those who own the equipment. This may be a commercial organization or another educational institution already embarked on telecommunications.

Consortia are a growing solution to sharing the high costs of videoconferencing, or the teaching and expert resources of a range of educational institutions. Another resource-sharing solution to high costs is the joint use of study centres. In some places these are called 'telecottages', in which various kinds of teaching media are at the disposal of the local community. As competition amongst educational providers increases, these telecottages will allow students to access courses from a variety of sources and will offer a wider market for niche courses.

Implications for the future

The considerations discussed so far are concerned with the present and with the way education and training are currently taking place. Predictions are, however, that education and training will change in response to various social and economic pressures. Multimedia desktop conferencing, which combines these three technologies and others, will be the facilitator of this change.

Training needs to move away from the concept of an event during which work stops, to an ongoing activity which combines with work (see Figure 3.2). Competence must be acquired in an evolutionary way. The idea of the expert teacher must give way to a network of supports and resources in which everyone has some kind of expertise to be tapped. Education and training increasingly need to be:

- distributed, over time and place;
- multi-sensory, to involve the whole person;
- interruptable, by work, leisure and personal commitments;
- transferable across cultures.

Photo courtesy of PictureTel

Figure 3.2 *Desktop conferencing combines work and training*

The idea of an educational course needs to be completely re-conceived – from a two-day event to a two-minute interchange. It must be modular, portable, non-linear and responsive. While educational institutions will still be needed, their form and operation need to change. For example, there is no need for some organizations to be rooted in time and place – they can be electronic, distributed and multicultural, just as some courses are currently.

As we move towards this future, we must reconsider how courses are developed, stored, delivered and managed. Desktop systems will support online help facilities, tutorials, browsing tools, and search and reference facilities. These will all put the user centre-stage as manager of the learning process. Teachers have just as important a role in this new future, but it is as preparer of material, facilitator of interaction, expert in how to find, access and use information. Many of the skills necessary to bring this vision of the educational future to reality can be developed through the use of the present three communications technologies.

References

Barker, B and Goodwin, R (1992) 'Audiographics: Linking remote classrooms', *The Computing Teacher*, April.

Burge, E and Roberts, J (1993) *Classrooms with a Difference. A practical guide to the use of conferencing technologies,* Toronto: Ontario Institute for Studies in Education.

Davie, L (1989) 'Facilitation techniques for the on-line tutor', in Mason, R and Kaye, A R (eds) *Mindweave: Communication, computers and distance education*, Oxford: Pergamon.

Deacon, B (1993) *Supporting Remote Students. Distance education, the Open University and the remote learner*, Bristol: The Open University, South West Region.

Gunawardena, C (1992) 'Changing faculty roles for audiographics and online teaching', *The American Journal of Distance Education*, **6**, 3, 58–71.

Lange, J (1993) 'ISDN videoconferencing for education and training', in Mason, R and Bacsich, P (eds) *ISDN Applications in Education and Training*, London: Institution of Electrical Engineers.

Maloy, W and Perry, N (1991) 'A navy video teletraining project: lessons learned', *The American Journal of Distance Education*, **5**, 3.

Rawlings, A *et al.* (1993) 'Telematic Networks for Open and Distance Learning in the Tertiary Sector. Volume 1. Scenarios, Costings and Survey', CCAM Deliverable, Brussels: European Commission.

Rumble, G (1989) 'On-line costs: Interactivity at a price', in Mason, R and Kaye, A R (eds) *Mindweave: Communication, computers and distance education*, Oxford: Pergamon.

Chapter 4

Computer conferencing

Conferencing systems

Conferencing software varies somewhat in its functionalities from one system to another, but most have the following features:

- electronic mail to one or more individuals on the system;
- conferences in which a set of participants can read and write a group of messages;
- subconferences within conferences so that different topics of discussion can be distinguished;
- user information such as details about participants, lists of conferences, dates of last log ons, search facilities for particular messages;
- levels of privilege, for initiating conferencing, moderating conferences, removing messages, reading only or reading and writing messages in particular conferences.

Other attributes of a few systems are: the facility to make anonymous or pseudonymous contributions; to use synchronous chat facilities; to make connections to other mail and conferencing systems, and to support online exams and assignments. Newer systems allow voice, formatted or graphical attachments to messages.

There are a number of other ways of communicating to groups of people electronically: electronic mail, bulletin boards, and distribution lists. One of the key elements of a conferencing system, however, is the structure provided for grouping messages. New members can read messages sent before they joined the system and anyone can reread already-seen messages. This supports the feeling of a group networked together by a common collection of messages. Distribution lists simply send mail messages to a registered group of participants. As these messages appear along with other electronic mail, there is no need to log into a special conferencing system. This has advantages in convenience, but disadvantages in creating a learning environment. Bulletin board systems used to be distinguished from conferencing systems by their very simplified conference structure and lack of user information. Electronic mail systems used to offer simple one-to-one or one-to-many messaging without retrieval ability. However, as all these systems evolve, the differences are blurring.

Although the main commercially available systems, such as COM, Participate and CoSy are very large, complex programs, simplified versions are not difficult to design and write. Consequently the amount of software available worldwide, some of it freeware, is very extensive. Many institutions have their own in-house systems, and others use very simple messaging systems which fulfil their needs at a very modest price. Some systems even come free with the hardware.

Deciding which system to use, therefore, requires considerable investigation of the market and, more importantly, a careful analysis of the purpose and needs it is to fulfil.

The interface

Because conferencing systems need to be accessed by a range of machines, from terminals to Macs and from standard PCs to non-standard machines, the interface has, until recently, remained very primitive. Facilities have to work for machines of the lowest common denominator.

Commands and responses are rarely intuitive; as Figure 4.1 shows, the command to write a message in CoSy is 'say'. For new and occasional users it is hard to remember all the terms from one session to the next. However, interfaces with menus and automatic log on facilities have been available for some time, and these have improved usability, particularly for distance students working without local support. Recent developments such as Windows have made a very significant improvement in the usability of the latest conferencing systems. As Figure 4.2 shows, various screens are nested in 'Windows', so that changing from one area to another simply requires clicking on a particular screen, rather than typing in a word. Furthermore, messages can be viewed in summary form which gives an overview of content and contributors. Again, these can be selected simply by clicking on the required message box.

Research is just beginning on the effects of these friendlier systems on the educational process. Will ease of learning and using the system lead to more active and interactive participants? While it is hard to expect anything

```
* * *  CoSy VMS v2.03 [OU Version]  * * *

              Copyright University of Guelph
     Implemented by Disus, a Division of TSB International, Inc.

You have mail messages: 1 new, 2 hold, 2 out and 0 ack
You are a member of 64 conference(s) and 2 conversations.

Mail:status
----------------------------NEW MAIL----------------------------------
 1 rd_mason      268106  15-Nov-93 16:47 conference plans
----------------------------OUT BASKET--------------------------------
 2 c-cooper      268102  15-Nov-93 16:36 OET write up
 3 rd_mason      268106  15-Nov-93 16:47 conference plans
----------------------------HOLD BASKET-------------------------------
 4 ar_kaye       266006  25-Oct-93 11:57 OET94 : OU costs
 5 am-pincas     266843   2-Nov-93 08:10 Textbook for the course

Mail:show oet2
Moderator    : ar_kaye
Description  : Tutor conference for the OET93 Course
Status       : Closed, read and write
Created      : 04-Jan-93 11:11
Last Modified : 15-Nov-93 16:40
-----------------------------------------------------------------------
discuss      for discussion of course design issues      0/295 *
guide        contributions to the oet94 Course Guide       0/35
oet94        general discussion of oet94 course            0/6
Read-Only topics are flagged with an '*'

Read: join oet2
Topics are 'discuss', 'guide', 'oet94'.

Topic? guide
Joining conference 'oet2', topic 'guide'. 0 new message(s) of 35.

No more unread messages in this topic.
Press <RETURN> for next active conference/topic.

Read:say
TITLE: My contribution
Enter Text. End with '.<CR>' or '(q)uit'
>My contribution to the guide consists of the following:
>    a list of aims and objectives
>    a reading list
```

Figure 4.1 *A command line conferencing system*

but positive improvements, evaluators of conferencing applications have always concluded that the technology is not the problem. Social and pedagogical issues play by far the bigger part in the creation of a successful learning environment.

The considerable interest in collaborative practices in business and education has led software designers to develop new facilities to support online group work. While systems now exist for joint project writing, joint document editing, and appending comments to documents, these facilities are not yet integrated with conferencing systems, except in rare instances.

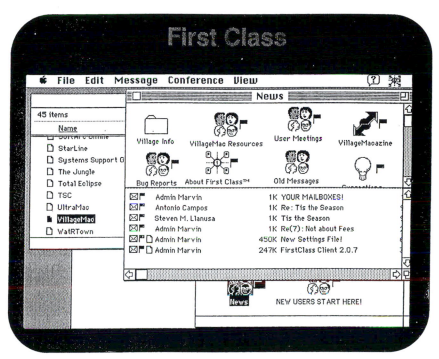

Figure 4.2 *A conferencing system using Windows*

This will undoubtedly be one of the benefits of multimedia desktop conferencing. In the meantime, collaborative activities with computer conferencing tend to centre around discussion and very simple project work. Improvements to conferencing systems in support of collaboration do exist however, and they can be summarized as facilities which enhance the telepresence of the group, that is, the sense of interacting with real people:

- easier means of getting an overview of the group members, the conferences, the new and old messages;
- appropriate means of defining and setting boundaries around the group and its activities.

Tools for teachers to manage student assignments, to take polls of student opinion and to monitor their contributions, are also recent innovations to some systems.

Most users who access conferencing systems via a modem want to be able to download messages onto their machine, either to print out or read offline. Even those who access the system via a local area network with no telephone charges may want to prepare their messages offline on a word-processor, rather than use the primitive editor in the conferencing system. These editors usually do not word-wrap at the end of a line, do not allow 'cut and paste', and certainly do not spell-check. Some users, however, prefer the 'buzz' of working online; they feel more connected with the group. The software and expertise necessary to work offline adds another level of difficulty for novice users. Front-end software, which acts as a buffer between the user and the conferencing software, is available for many systems to automate these procedures and, to some extent, to mimic the conferencing system on the user's machine.

Metaphors, such as the campus, schoolhouse or classroom, are often used to help new students conceptualize the 'space' of a conferencing system, and to find their way around the various facilities. Conferences are usually presented as rooms, with each room forming the setting for a specific activity or topic of discussion. One conference may be designated as a seminar room, another as a café, a third as a help space for requesting or volunteering assistance. The metaphor helps users to see that they move from room to room by changing conferences.

Ultimately, the aim of all telecommunications media is to be transparent, so that the learner is most conscious of the content of the communication, not the equipment or the means of communication. In some sense, computer conferencing has a very long way to go in achieving transparency. Even with the newest software, the user still needs some awareness of telecommunications, some understanding of personal computing and often a great deal of ingenuity with troubleshooting problems on their own equipment. On the other hand, when conferencing is working transparently, the lack of 'interference' by the physical presence and characteristics of the teacher and other students leads to considerable concentration on the content of the communication – perhaps more so than with any other medium. The particular form of telepresence created through computer conferencing – a disembodied form of presence compared with the other two media – is a powerful element in the experience of this medium, although it does not appeal to all users.

Types of educational uses

Although the range of educational uses of computer conferencing are vast, most of them fall into the following categories.

- *Optional or add-on uses*

This category includes most uses in schools for inter-class, inter-institutional and inter-cultural communication. At tertiary level, it includes tutorial support for distance learners, online office hours for campus–based students, a delivery mechanism for assignments and comments, and a facility for student socializing and self-help groups. In the workplace, it includes a whole range of incidental learning arising from serendipitous contacts, and requests for help or information.

- *In conjunction with other media*

Computer conferencing is very often used in conjunction with other media as the delivery mechanism for part of the course. The rest of the course may be face–to–face teaching, print-based, or delivered by other sychronous media such as videoconferencing. For example, writing and communication courses use conferencing as a major teaching vehicle for peer comment and review. Second–language teaching often involves an online element to practice written language skills in a natural setting (sometimes with native speakers). Combining computer conferencing with audioconferencing is another possibility. The synchronicity of telephone discussion allows the group to sort out 'who will do what' much more efficiently, and to arrive at decisions more effectively. Conferencing can be used for the initial exploration or design phase of a project involving distributed groups, or to discuss set reading material on an otherwise distance education course. It is used to keep students in touch with the teacher and each other in between monthly meetings, whether face-to-face or via teleconference.

- *As the primary delivery mechanism*

The number of online courses is increasing steadily as access to equipment improves in many countries. Although online courses almost always include some print material, in the form of a set book, articles to be downloaded from online databases or a tailor-made study guide, the primary focus of the course is the discussions, activities and seminars to be carried out on the conferencing system. Courses such as this exist at all levels of the curriculum, from primary to PhD level, internationally and for the local community, in training, professional updating and continuing education fields. Entire programmes of study are available from a few institutions, particularly at undergraduate and Master's degree levels.

Depending on the type of use, students' log on rates will range from daily to monthly. Some may never actually initiate a message, at least in a conference; others will be expected to contribute regularly. The type of use will also affect the desirable number of participants in any conference. Eight students in an online course sending a message every day will soon create a large conference. Two hundred students using a system optionally, and mostly reading rather than writing, may be necessary to make a conference viable. With groups of 30–50, some plenary conferences are probably useful, as long as they are supplemented by small group conferences in which the subsets carry out the majority of their interactive discussions. There are many ways of dividing up groups; for example, a pair can begin a discussion, then join with another pair to compare results, prepare a joint view and present it to the whole group. Alternatively, one group can be given the task of explaining an issue or viewpoint to another group.

The 'master class' model is also applicable to computer conferencing. This works particularly well with a guest lecturer or outside expert and a large group of students. Discussion, often sparked off by a structured input from the 'master', takes place with a few of the participants, who probably self-select. The rest of the group read the messages – and may even discuss some of the implications in other conferences, or reference extracts from the master class in their assignments.

An increasing number of large organizations, many of them multi-national, run their own electronic mail and conferencing systems. These systems support various formal work groups within the organization, but also provide a network of human resources which are the prototype of the future learning environment. Staff who require information not available locally, or who have a problem of some sort, can put out a message requesting advice or information. These messages frequently begin, 'Does anyone know ...?'. Studies show that people are very willing to respond to such messages, or to refer them on to someone who does know. Responses within hours provide a corporate resource which has no equal, both for improved productivity and for staff development.

> Another aspect of conferencing which contributes to its learning potential is its constant availability at the place of work. It is not necessary to make special arrangements to 'get at' some knowledge – one doesn't even have to leave one's desk. That means that people can consult the information pool anytime they need to know something. If and when they get an answer through conferencing, it can be immediately applied in the work situation which provoked the question (Gundry, 1992, p. 172).

This type of use seems more consistent with the general principles of adult learning than most formal education and training situations provide. The use of conferencing amongst teachers, researchers and other academics parallels this informal use in organizations. Learning is a sometimes unnoticed by-product of networking, socializing and information exchanges which are common in collegial interaction online.

Advantages of computer conferencing

Interactivity is undoubtedly the major advantage of computer conferencing, and this is supported and enhanced by the ability to interact after time for reflection rather than on-the-spot. The textual nature of the interaction has a number of educational advantages: it develops written communication skills; it enhances in-depth processing and recall of course material; and it prepares students for examinations which demand written expression of responses.

Collaborative discussions and peer activities are also a positive feature this medium facilitates, particularly for distance education. Brainstorming, seminar discussion, small group work and peer learning are examples of this.

The encouragement this medium provides to develop the independence and self-directed approach of the learner is another of its most often cited advantages. The model which successful conferences project is that of active learners engaging in the construction of meaning.

On-the-job training and informal learning through networking are both significant advantages of the medium in the workplace. Although training handbooks and educational literature have been saying it for some time, both organizations and educational institutions are now beginning to realize that the expertise of other learners is a vastly under-used resource in most formal education.

Social conferences are invariably the first to take off, and usually contain by far the most messages of any form of conference. Evaluators continually refer to the beneficial aspects of this facility for the educational process:

> The popularity of the electronic socialising form leaves no doubt that participation in conferences has a beneficial effect on motivation. There is evidence indicating a positive relationship between participation in conferences and course completion or success in the final examination. The importance of the social dimension of computer mediated communication should not be overlooked. Students get a sense of belonging as a result of participation (Soby, 1992, p. 43).

The democratic and equalizing tendency of computer conferencing has often been noted. Conferencing empowers grassroots discussions and even subverts traditional power structures. Access is the essence of the medium, not status (see, for example, Mason, 1993).

Inter-cultural activities are another bonus of computer conferencing at all levels, from schools to organizations. No other medium so facilitates interaction amongst people from different cultural backgrounds. This is partly because writing in a second language is easier than speaking.

Community-based education through telecottages in remote areas and through electronic city programmes in both industrialized and developing countries has also been extended by computer conferencing.

In some contexts, conferencing facilitates a kind of intimacy and personal openness that makes it very suitable for counselling, self-development and other support mechanisms (Johnson-Lenz and Johnson-Lenz, 1991). The virtual community, which has many of the emotionally satisfying characteristics of the physical community, is considered by some to be the most important contribution of computer conferencing to the present age (Rheingold, 1993).

Finally, computer conferencing supports the aims of most humanistic educational programmes:

> If effective teaching and learning call for a way and a place to express and explore interests, to raise and respond to questions, to discover, practise and experiment with ideas and cognitive skills, to identify and examine relevant information and ideas, and to broaden and deepen individual ways of thinking about the world by providing the opportunity to consider and evaluate alternative views both privately and through interactive 'live' discussions, then certainly CMC [computer-mediated communication] more than qualifies (Marantz and England, 1993).

Computer conferencing's unique contribution to the educational scene is that it combines written communication with interaction. The fact that the interaction is time-independent adds to the reflective quality of the medium.

This list of advantages might leave the novice wondering why computer conferencing has not taken over the entire educational establishment. A look at the following disadvantages will balance the picture.

Disadvantages of computer conferencing

Most of the advantages of computer conferencing have disadvantages bound up intimately with them. For example, the much vaunted time for reflection produces no pressure to respond and the silence in many conferences is deafening! On the other hand, the equal opportunity for all to express their opinions can lead to chaos and an overwhelming number of messages. While the textual nature of the medium has educational advantages, writing takes longer to produce and to read than speech. All in all, most people find conferencing a time-consuming activity.

The asynchronicity of conferencing, and particularly the notion that students can come in at any point and make their comment, is somewhat suspect. Many reports suggest that in dynamic conferences, the keenest students jump in straight away, often with very competent or literate responses. Less confident students, or those who are not able to log on frequently, find that the discussion has always moved on or others have already made their point. The following are extracts from student messages (from OET course, case study 1 in Chapter 7):

> I download the messages and print them out to read on the train, mentally composing my uniquely brilliant contribution walking home from the station. The next day I log on, find there are x number of new messages, read them first and discover others have already made my points. I print out all the new messages to read on the train ....

> I had no idea I was going to find it so hard to join in – I have composed numerous messages off-line only to chicken out after reading other comments, better written, more concise than my own.

> I am discovering that unless I can enter the conversation with points relating to discussions going on between those of our group who contribute regularly, my messages do not receive any comments.

Just as in face-to-face meetings, a small number dominate the interaction. Although potentially anyone can put in a message about any subject at any time, the dynamics of online discussion are not as different from face-to-face discussion as the potential would allow.

When teachers find conferencing an exciting and fulfilling medium to work with, their enthusiasm and efforts usually produce successful conferences. With mediocre teachers who lack social and communications skills, who are unwilling to spend the time to facilitate discussion, or who retain authoritarian views of education, conferencing does not work. The medium is very dependent on the teacher setting an appropriate climate and structure for interaction.

If the medium is demanding for teachers, it is more so for students. Many have not experienced the demands of interactive learning in their educational careers, or they may have been steeped in the philosophy of competition and learning in isolation. They may be facing a whole new approach to education in computer conferencing, and this will inevitably take time to establish. Others may favour the idea of interacting through computer conferencing, but in practice lack time, confidence or effort. Most evaluation reports contain a litany of reasons from students for their unresponsiveness.

Even when conferencing is working well with active and interactive participants, it is still a poor medium for a range of activities. Foremost among these are decision-making processes or group consensus; conferencing is good for divergent not convergent thinking. (When conferencing merges with the synchronous voice and visual media, both types of group process – brain storming and decision making – will find support.)

The lack of focus on personal characteristics in conferencing is advantageous in many ways, but it is also blamed for the phenomenon known as 'flaming', the term for an online row. The literature abounds with references to these overheated discussions, usually arising from a misunderstanding.

> One of the functions for which conferencing is justifiably lauded, is its facility for providing feedback, for allowing people who would normally be disenfranchised, to express their opinions, for making accessible people who are usually aloof or unavailable. It must, therefore, be accepted that this facility carries with it the freedom for people to express negative, unpopular and dissenting views which may have been repressed or unheard for a very long time. This is particularly true in education where students' views on anything but the actual content of the course are rarely solicited or expressed openly. Now this fact certainly does not account for all the online rows, but there is a sense of release felt by new and experienced conferencers alike, that here is a vehicle like no other, for speaking one's mind (Mason, 1993, p. 10)

Organizational studies of the medium report the same double-edged sword of advantage and disadvantage arising from the freedom and democracy of conferencing operating in hierarchical structures.

Finally, while conferencing has empowered many previously disenfranchised groups, the barriers to access caused by the necessary equipment and communications infrastructure continue to exacerbate the divide between the 'haves' and 'have-nots'. The cost of telephone charges for distance students to access the system is yet another barrier.

Future trends

The future of computer conferencing is undoubtedly one of great mergers – with synchronous media, with multimedia, with the whole panoply of desktop facilities. Some would say, the sooner the better! While this merger is already happening at the leading edge with integrated text, sound and graphics being exchanged on higher speed modems, the growth area for text-only communication lies with the Internet and access to a whole range of library resources. The role of the online teacher will increasingly be that of guide to these resources. It will be interesting to see what needs computer conferencing fulfils with the advent of cheap audio and visual connections. If messages remain asynchronous (like telephone answering machines), will text be relegated to formal papers and documents? Will the stimulation of voice and visual communication overcome learners' inertia and be more compelling to respond to than text?

Another trend predicted to continue is international online connections – for example, collaborations amongst students studying similar courses at different institutions. School children carrying out multicultural investigations are a powerful and inexpensive resource for extending the classroom walls.

> It would be naive to think that communication will automatically lead to greater knowledge, increased respect for individual and cultural differences, and a new appreciation of similarities. But a more peaceful world will not evolve without communication. The technology of CMC does not lead directly to the answers, but the dialogue it supports is a significant way for people to begin to embrace the common questions (Wells, 1993, p. 85).

As 'pure' computer conferencing falls increasingly towards the trailing edge of technology, it will continue to find specialist uses in education and training. Old computer equipment will be perfectly adequate for textual communication, and could be used with those who currently cannot afford access. By comparison with multimedia conferencing, computer conferencing will be an inexpensive technology, which will continue to grow at grass-roots level.

In the short term, conferencing systems with improved interfaces will find increasing markets, and learners will increasingly have to adapt to the interactive and collaborative paradigm they represent. However, this technology-led growth will eventually meet a new generation of users reared with the computer and schooled in international communication and then tele-learning will become the norm rather than the exception.

References

Gundry, J (1992) 'Understanding collaborative learning in networked organisations', in Kaye, A R (ed.) *Collaborative Learning Through Computer Conferencing. The Najaden papers*, Berlin: Springer-Verlag.

Johnson-Lenz, P and Johnson-Lenz, T (1991) 'Post-mechanistic group-ware primitives: Rhythms, boundaries and containers. *International Journal of Man-Machine Studies*, **34**, 3, 395–418.

Marantz, B and England, R (1993) 'Can CMC teach teachers training?', *EMI*, **30**, 2, 74–7.

Mason, R (ed.) (1993) *Computer Conferencing: The last word*, Victoria, BC: Beach Holme Publications.

Rheingold, H (1993) 'Virtual communities', in Mason, R (ed.) *Computer Conferencing: The last word*, Victoria, BC: Beach Holme Publications.

Soby, M (1992) 'Waiting for electropolis', in Kaye, A R (ed.) *Collaborative Learning Through Computer Conferencing. The Najaden papers*, Berlin: Springer-Verlag.

Wells, R (1993) 'The use of computer-mediated communication in distance education: progress, problems and trends', in Davies, G and Samways, B (eds) *Teleteaching*, Proceedings of the IFIP TC3 Third Teleteaching Conference, Trondheim, Norway. Amsterdam: North-Holland.

Chapter 5

Audiographics

Equipment

Audiographics systems consist of two parts: audio equipment and computer graphics software and equipment. Much of the following description of audio systems is as applicable to pure audioconferencing as it is to audiographics.

Audio

The aim of any voice communication system is to pick up and transmit a strong, clear sound of the users' voices. Background sounds, which in face-to-face communication the listener can easily distinguish from direct speech, are the major nuisance in transmitted sound. Typical background sounds come from fluorescent lights, computer cooling fans, extraneous conversation, coughing and paper rustling. Hollow sounding reverberation comes from hard surfaces in the room. Choosing the right audio system for an application depends on a number of contextual factors: the acoustics of the room, the type of conference and degree of interactivity required, and the positioning of the participants.

The ordinary telephone is the normal solution for audioconferencing when each participant is in a different location. When a group of students in one room participates in an audioconference, a speakerphone is the normal solution. This has an internal, omnidirectional microphone, which responds equally to all sounds from all directions. Students must be seated at a uniform distance around a table close to the microphone. For audiographics, a telephone headset with integral microphone for each student is ideal, as it provides perfect voice pickup and a barrier to background noise. When any ordinary telephone-based system is used to connect the various sites, normal conversation amongst all participants can take place interactively and simultaneously. With half-duplex systems, only one person can speak at a time; any other person speaking will be cut off. This has advantages and disadvantages – no confusing over-talking can develop, but on the other hand, turn-taking can be very stilted and formalized.

Similarly, microphones with push-to-talk buttons require users to activate the microphone manually when they want to speak. This is called a closed system, because the microphone does not transmit sound until activated. An open microphone system is one which picks up multiple sound sources using a microphone that is active (open) all the time. Many students feel that closed systems inhibit normal communication and interaction, imposing a formality and lack of spontaneity which is undesirable. However, closed systems are frequently used, and one advantage is that groups can discuss matters amongst themselves before switching on their microphone to put a question from the group.

Audiographics

The graphics side of this medium is analagous to an overhead projector, in that everyone shares the same view. The difference is that with audiographics, this view can be changed or manipulated by any of the sites. Apart from various peripheral equipment, the essential elements of a system are: a computer and screen, audiographics software, a graphics tablet or light pen, and a modem. Additional components depend on the application, but can include a printer, a scanner, a large screen monitor and a video card. Graphics can be prepared with drawing software or can be scanned in from such sources as videos, slides, pictures, 3D objects and transparencies.

As with audio, multi-site audiographics connections require an audiobridge and, in addition, a databridge. This can sometimes be accommodated by one of the machines on the system. With some products, all sites have equal control and may change the shared screen; with others, one site controls any changes to the screen.

A graphics tablet consists of a flat pad with a pen attached by a wire. As the pen is drawn across the tablet, the mark appears on the computer screen (not the tablet). This means that the user must look at the screen for direct feedback from the hand's movement (see Figure 5.2). Most people learn this skill with a little practice. The alternative is a light pen which allows the user to draw directly onto the computer screen (see Figure 5.1). This

Photo courtesy of Fujitsu

Figure 5.1 *Use of a light pen*

notion of a pen and a shared screen gave rise to the earliest term for audiographics systems, 'electronic whiteboard'. The simplest systems are still basically a shared drawing or writing board. Multimedia desktop systems, however, are increasingly more sophisticated, offering video capability, document sharing and access to resources such as computer-based training programs and databases. Nevertheless, despite the video and the other gee-whizz features, the essence of these new facilities remains the interactivity around a shared graphical space.

Software

There are several audiographics systems which currently dominate the education market. Facilities vary a little from one system to another – for example, the way in which control of the whiteboard is handled.

Figure 5.2 from the VIS-A-VIS audiographics system shows the shared screen and the facilities on the side.

The Macintosh audiographics system (used in case study 4; see chapter 7) has 'status indicator' lamps on the screen, so that the teacher may pass control of the screen to any site by simply clicking on their status lamp.

Photo courtesy of VIS-A-VIS

Figure 5.2 *An audiographics system*

Fujitsu's system provides 'flipcharts' for brainstorming, note taking and annotation of any screen, by either keyboard, mouse or lightpen.

Types of educational uses

Audiographics is really a hybrid medium, whose roots lie in audioconferencing. The most significant educational uses of audioconferencing are for remote delivery of classroom instruction and for tutorial support of distance education students. When remote sites consist of a group of students, one is sometimes designated to act as spokesperson.

In the training sector, audioconferencing has taken a back-seat role to videoconferencing. However, there are signs of a revival of interest in the wake of the principle 'use the simplest technology which works, not the most sophisticated which can be afforded'.

In some instances, people are looking at video and finding that it's an overkill or not the mechanism they wish to use to reach a large number of sites. In these instances, audio is coming back into light (*ETF News*, 1993).

For example, the Bank of America uses audioconferencing for product training to help stimulate cross-selling activity throughout Europe. A product specialist links into all the division's offices and makes a focused presentation. Written material is distributed in advance so that all participants can use the same reference text. Occasionally, two speakers share the presentations, which usually last about an hour. Tapes of the sessions are made and used by those who were unavailable for the live training.

Audiographics systems add a focal point to the audio discussion. Even in cases where very little interactive use is made of the graphics facility, this focus for pointing and highlighting contributes significantly to the telepresence of the group (Tuckey, 1993).

Audiographics systems can be used with larger groups to deliver lectures. An enlarged screen monitor projects the shared image to the remote site(s) and the voice of the lecturer can be heard and annotations, pointing and changes to the image can be seen. Students can ask questions via the audio link.

More often, audiographics systems are used to connect small groups at remote locations for tutorial interactions. In this model, the audiographics medium is analogous to the classroom rather than the lecture hall, and is highly interactive. It is particularly useful for problem-solving curricula and peer learning situations.

> Because of the equipment needed for audiographic communication, most experiences involve groups of learners clustered around a computer, or a graphics pad, or collectively viewing a projected image of a computer screen, in a specially equipped centre (in contrast to many audioconferencing situations, which can easily involve individual participants using their own telephone). This group context – which may involve several groups in multi-site systems, including a group physically co-present with the teacher – introduces a fairly complex communicative situation, mixing telepresence with real presence (Kaye, 1993).

Uses of audiographics systems are particularly numerous within primary and secondary school systems to link remote schools to larger centres of expertise and resources, for example, in the UK, Australia, Canada and the USA. Distance teaching programmes which are based around study centres are also frequent users of audiographics systems for providing tutorial support and an interactive element to print-based education and training. Community-level schemes providing adult continuing education are often secondary uses of audiographics systems in remote locations. Similarly, training applications are often piggybacked onto general management communications facilities. In other cases they are a product of collaborative programmes between universities and industry to provide on-the-job training.

Audiographics systems are particularly favoured by administrators who see this technology as a cost-effective way of meeting the demand for equal provision in remote areas. Many current audiographics programmes at all levels have two to six students at a number of sites in very remote areas, for example, in Alaska, northern Ontario, Queensland in Australia, Scandinavian countries, and the Highlands and Islands of Scotland. Certainly the alternatives of either videoconferencing or sending out tutors are much more costly.

Apart from school-based uses, audiographics systems are generally accessed from study centres. These may be part of community centres or telecottages, or they may be located in the local library. Home-based systems are said to be 'just around the corner', but no applications currently involve students at home. (A partial exception is case study 6, Chapter 7.)

A number of state or province-wide programmes have adopted audiographics systems as the basis for extending education to a wider population (for example, New Brunswick in Canada). Equipment has been installed throughout the area, and is used by secondary schools, university distance education units, professional training institutions and community education providers.

In a distance education application, audiographics sessions provide the interactivity and contact which the package of correspondence materials lacks. Visuals used during the sessions can be catalogued and archived so that they can be retrieved the next time the course is offered. The 'live' sessions provide a vehicle for updating the printed material of the course, as well as enhancing the educational potential of particularly visual or auditory areas of the curriculum, such as fine arts, geography, mathematics and language learning.

Advantages of audiographics systems

An audiographics system provides an environment for emulating the face-to-face tutorial and can offer all the advantages of conventional small group work to learners at a distance. The system offers and encourages a high level of interactivity between student and teacher, and seems to increase student motivation and completion of courses. Perhaps the most positive accolade of this medium is that users often do not comment on it in their feedback about audiographics-based courses. In short, it is relatively transparent to the teaching process.

School teachers like audiographics for its relatively 'low-tech' (compared to satellite-based TV, for instance) approach to increasing access. It also allows the school and the individual teacher to maintain local control of the process, whereas central distribution of teaching often means loss of control.

Proponents of the medium say that the emphasis on sharing and working with a set of documents is a more focused and educationally beneficial facility than seeing the teacher and participants, whose physical appearance and mannerisms can be distracting. Furthermore, dialogue is more natural and spontaneous than the formal question and answer sessions of many videoconferencing applications. Although it is important for teachers to vary the tone and modulation of their voice, audiographics courses are less dependent on the charisma or personality of the teacher than videoconferences.

Many teachers report that students' work produced on audiographics courses is of a higher standard than comparable work in traditional classes. This is particularly so with group projects.

> In spite of the frustrations students experienced while working at a distance on group projects, the quality of the group research papers and presentations was outstanding. The group projects were of a much higher quality than the individual position papers students completed. On the whole, they were also much more innovative and thought provoking than group projects completed in traditional classes. Part of this difference may be due to the fact that groups had to work much harder to communicate with each other and achieve a common goal. It was evident that group members learned from each other and complemented each other's strengths and weaknesses (Gunawardena, 1992).

Distance learners value the shortened turnaround time on assignments, when the system is used to scan in homework and subsequent feedback from the instructor. The long delays experienced by distance learners using postal delivery of assignments is a well-known disadvantage of correspondence systems.

Compared with computer conferencing and other computer-based systems, audiographics systems are relatively easy to operate and learn to use. This will be less true with multimedia desktop systems where each student will have to master the basic capabilities of the machine.

The audio and visual link means that teachers can employ a whole range of techniques for promoting discussion: brainstorming, panel discussions, group work, role playing and presentations by the students. Many teachers find the challenges presented by audiographics very stimulating and report that this has benefited their traditional face-to-face teaching.

Remote students benefit tremendously from the extended educational choice which audiographics provide. If either student or teacher has previously been obliged to travel long distances for courses, a reduction in travelling is almost always welcomed.

Because the medium involves small groups at any one site, it is ideal for professional updating of a number of staff at an organization or school. Providing training to groups of professionals from the same workplace creates many opportunities for enhancing collaborative relationships and long-term working arrangements.

Audiographics systems are finding new markets in business, particularly those with distributed sites or international partners. Desktop systems are more convenient and economical than videoconferencing, allowing short multi-site conferences without a lot of planning in advance. Training and professional updating are a natural extension of the use of the facilities. Training programmes are always well accepted when they are integrated with the working environment and use familiar tools. The fact that this medium is synchronous means that the trainee must set aside a specific time for the training session. Computer conferencing courses in which the participants use workplace equipment often lead to conflicts, as no specific time has to be allocated to the training.

Although true costs of educational media are notoriously difficult to untangle, there is no doubt that many educational institutions are reporting that audiographics systems are very cost-effective in a variety of applications (see, for example, Smith, 1992). Compared with videoconferencing or with sending instructors on site, audiographics is considered equally effective and much cheaper. The start-up costs are relatively low and additional equipment can be added incrementally. Ongoing operation costs are usually limited to the telephone charges.

Any participating site can be the primary delivery node, so that not only can students make presentations, but also any site can both deliver and receive instruction. Furthermore, those systems which operate over ordinary telephone lines allow linkages anywhere in the world.

The essence of audiographics is the shared screen which any participant can alter. The most enduring uses of the medium will exploit this capability.

Disadvantages of audiographics systems

Audiographics, like videoconferencing systems, are only as good as the audio link. That is, the quality and reliability of the audio is the major determinant of users' perception of the medium. The class can continue without the graphics or the video link, but not without the audio. While there is rarely any complaint about the technical aspect of the graphics or software, the same cannot be said of the audio. Extraneous noise or interference on the line can cause voice transmission on speaker phones to become unintelligible. Sometimes the link to one or even all sites is unaccountably disconnected during a session. Teachers need to make contingency plans for possible losses of the audio link, and seating arrangements at remote sites need to provide equal and adequate access to the microphone. Although audio systems are improving, as are the telephone networks they depend on, the poor quality of sound has in the past accounted for the failure of some audiographics applications.

The teacher's role in audiographics courses is undoubtedly time-consuming. First of all, there is the planning of each session. As it is very much more difficult to teach on the fly than in a face-to-face class, it is important to prepare a detailed 'storyboard' of the whole session. Secondly, it is necessary to consider what strategies to use to encourage interaction and group work. Finally, and most time-consuming of all, there is the preparation of visual material. If no assistance is provided by the institution, the teacher must also master any software necessary for producing drawings, pictures or other scanned material. With most systems, the slides to be used are sent to the remote sites in advance of the session, so that valuable teaching time is not wasted in downloading material. Consequently, all of this planning and preparation must be carried out by the teacher well before the actual session.

Although audiographics systems are easy to use, there is still a need for some level of support, particularly at remote sites. Training and maintenance of the equipment are important at the technical level, and group facilitation and course administration may also be necessary, depending on the context of the application.

Despite these disadvantages, what is most remarkable about audio-graphics systems is how few drawbacks they have.

Lack of awareness

Unlike computer conferencing and videoconferencing, there is relatively little literature on audiographics applications, much less any research on course design or educational outcomes. This is possibly because audiographic conferencing is mainly used in small group situations and lacks the 'scaleability' of the other two media. While this is a positive attribute of the medium for educators, it does not offer an obvious solution to the increasing pressure to provide life-long learning for everyone.

Audiographics as a medium also seems to lack glamour – the students are not as isolated as home-based computer conferencing users, and the teachers are not performers, as in videoconferencing. Although educational applications and sales of equipment are undoubtedly growing worldwide, there is a curious disregard for the medium. While academics and practitioners endlessly debate the merits and demerits of video and computer conferencing, users of audiographics simply get on with teaching and learning. There is a grass-roots, 'low tech' attitude to audiographics that belies its success and penetration of the education and training scene. This lack of awareness of the medium and its benefits may be inevitable. Its ancestor – audioconferencing – is equally ignored in the face of more leading-edge technologies.

Future trends

If audiographics systems, as such, have a lack-lustre past, their future promises much greater recognition – although not with the same name. A shared whiteboard is the central feature of multimedia desktop systems, despite the video and text-based facilities. Because document conferencing can be carried out over conventional phone lines and without expensive hardware additions, it is likely to become prevalent far sooner than desktop video. In fact, most desktop videoconferencing systems give equal weight to the shared screen as to the video window.

Currently, these systems are beginning to penetrate the business market, and are primarily used in one-to-one conferencing rather than in multi-site discussions. Training applications in which each participant has a machine on their desk are rare, but the potential is enormous. Although the advantages of small co-located groups would be lost, the benefit of convenient access to training and local control of the learning environment will offer a challenging new area for educators and trainers.

Because of the cost-effectiveness and ease of use of current audiographics systems, their continued use, particularly in schools and remote learning situations, is probably assured for some time to come.

References

ETF News, Issue 5, Spring 1993.

Kaye, A R (1993) 'Co-learn: An ISDN-based multimedia environment', in Mason, R and Bacsich, P (eds) *ISDN Applications in Education and Training*, London: Institution of Electrical Engineers.

Gunawardena, C (1992) 'Changing faculty roles for audiographics and online teaching', *The American Journal of Distance Education*, **3**, 58-71.

Smith, T (1992) 'The evolution of audiographics teleconferencing for continuing engineering education at the University of Wisconsin-Madison', *International Journal for Continuing Engineering Education*, **2**, 2/3/4, 155–60.

Tuckey, C (1993) 'Computer conferencing and the electronic whiteboard in the United Kingdom: A comparative analysis', *The American Journal of Distance Education*, **7**, 2, 58–72.

Chapter 6

Videoconferencing

Equipment

A digital videoconferencing system consists of a video camera, a CODEC, a TV monitor and an audio unit. Usually these are combined into one cabinet. The video CODEC and audio unit convert the analogue video and audio signals from the video camera into a digital format. This digital data must also be compressed so that they can be sent through a digital communications link. The communications link may be through ISDN (basic rate or up to 384 kbits/s, or a leased data circuit operating up to 2 mbits/s).

Compression is handled in different ways, and it is this difference which leads to incompatibility between the various manufacturers. The H.261 compression algorithm conforms to a CCITT standard and should allow different brands of video CODEC to connect with each other. However, each CODEC manufacturer has their own proprietary algorithm which produces the best picture for their equipment, but will not inter-operate with another manufacturer's compression algorithm.

Most manufacturers produce a range of equipment from large room-size units with one monitor for the lecturer's face and another for the output from the graphics camera, to small desk-top versions with an integral camera. Figure 6.1 shows some models from VTEL's range.

If an ISDN link is installed, a terminal adapter unit is necessary to provide an interface between the video CODEC and the ISDN line. Charges for an ISDN line consist of a monthly rental and a usage rate equivalent to two standard telephone calls.

The room chosen for videoconferencing should reflect the number of students and the type of use. Lecture-style seating does not encourage informal interaction; a room which can accommodate a large number of

Photos courtesy of VTEL

Figure 6.1 *Desktop, rollabout and lecture-room videoconferencing equipment*

students is intimidating for a small group. Lighting levels in the room are also important. Too little light gives a poor picture quality, with colours looking faded and pronounced shadows giving a depressing feel to the image. An evenly-lit room is preferable to spot lights over the conference table, as this creates a more natural picture. The ideal table shape for a group of eight to ten students or trainees is thought to be trapezoidal, because it allows each participant to be visible to the camera and to each other, as well as to have access to writing space on the table. Multi-site videoconferences with just a few participants at each site usually have seats in a row.

Question and answer sessions after large lecture-style videoconferences usually require someone to pass a microphone around the hall to the questioner. Some purpose-built rooms have a push-to-talk microphone between two students which makes interaction somewhat more inviting. In systems where the camera position is activated by voice or by the push-to-talk button, the sense of the camera searching the room and then zooming in as a questioner speaks is slightly intimidating.

Bandwidth

The amount of bandwidth used to transmit the video image controls the resolution and motion rendition of the picture. A few studies have been carried out comparing various qualities of videoconferencing (for example, 128 kbits/s, 384 kbits/s and 2 mbits/s) and various levels of interaction (for example, two-way video, audio return, fax, telephone or email return). It is difficult to draw any firm conclusions about the educational value of these variations. Does it matter that the lecturer's movements are jerky and that lip synchronization with sound is not exact? As long as any graphical or textual material is legible, does slower speed of transmission matter? Certainly these factors add to the strain of videoconferences and do demand more attention. Regarding the level of interaction, students say that they prefer two-way interaction, although they may not make much use of it. Final results on examinations do not seem to indicate any difference. Most users are satisfied with the lower quality of video (128 kbits/s), given the high cost of providing near full motion videoconferencing at 2 mbits/s. Sound continuity is more important in any case.

A distinction should be drawn here between videoconferencing and educational television. For the latter, satellites are most commonly used to transmit video lectures to a large number of sites, with audio communication back from the sites. A number of major consortia exist in the USA to provide inter-institutional, inter-sector and international courses, particularly in the fields of engineering, technology, agriculture and telecommunications. The major advantage of satellite transmission is that the costs are independent of distance (within the area covered by the satellite) and costs can be spread over a large number of receiving sites. New digital satellite technology is changing this pattern, as full video interaction and transmissions to fewer sites are becoming cost-effective. Nevertheless, the advent of ISDN videoconferencing in the last few years is beginning to have an impact on the extensive one-way video systems which have taken root, particularly in the USA. For example, California State University, said to be the largest university system in the world, has recently moved over to digital videoconferencing from satellite technology in order to avoid initial costs of satellite time, to provide two-way interaction and to have easier access to an international audience.

Types of videoconferencing uses

By far the most commonly used type of videoconference course is the
'virtual' or 'candid' classroom. It most closely approximates a face-to-face
lecture or training session, except that some of the learners are not
physically present. It is essentially a didactic information presentation,
primarily by a lecturer talking directly to the camera, with illustrations and
possibly some interactions interspersed throughout. It takes place in a
specially equipped lecture room, with some students present and some at
one or more distant sites.

This format is most often used for state-of-the-art subject levels –
postgraduate courses or professional updating, or for presenting technical or
theoretical information. Its success, as with face-to-face lectures, depends
on a high level of student motivation, ability to take accurate notes and to
work with theoretical or technical material.

A slight variation of this format involves less lecturing and more
demonstrating or pre-prepared video presentation, for example of
equipment, laboratory experiments or dangerous procedures. In some
subjects, and particularly some training contexts, the facility to show what
could not be seen live is a strong justification for the medium. Figure 6.2

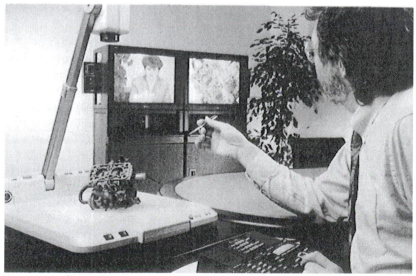

Photo courtesy of PictureTel

Figure 6.2 *Use of a document camera to transmit images of objects*

shows the use of a document camera to transmit images of objects. Applications in medical training are just one area in which videoconferencing is used to very great effect, for example, in giving medical students 'access' to operations.

Studio-produced videoconferences are another variant on the educational uses of this medium. In this situation, no students are actually present, and either the presenter lectures to a camera, or the format is closer to a conventional television programme. Examples include a studio discussion amongst several experts, or an adaptation of some visual footage with a voice-over commentary by the presenter.

Finally, there is a whole range of small group uses of videoconferencing, which may be point-to-point or multi-site. Due to the cost of equipment, many of these applications are subsidized by telephone companies or by bodies promoting equal opportunities in remote areas. Examples which really exploit the visual facility include teaching sign language to the deaf, in-service training for physical rehabilitation nurses, and training repairmen. Other applications use the medium to facilitate small group discussions in a typical seminar mode. A number of initiatives at the school level have been implemented to equalize access to specialized teaching in remote or rural areas.

The virtual or candid classroom model obviously demands the least adaptation on the part of the lecturer. At the other end of the scale, studio presentation or live demonstration requires considerable preparation and coordination amongst various parties. Small group videoconferences depend on the same facilitative skills as they do face-to-face. Nevertheless, regardless of the type of use, most institutions have had to cope with faculty resistance to its introduction. Many lecturers feel threatened by the medium, and the process of turning initial users into frequent and successful users is often slow (see case study 8, Chapter 7, for important factors in this process).

By far the majority of the uses of videoconferencing are in the training and postgraduate education fields. Undergraduate and school-based programmes usually involve educational television rather than videoconferencing, although this is changing rapidly. For example, in the USA, partnerships between local schools and business or industry use a two-way interactive cable network which provides a small-scale, locally controlled video interaction. Undergraduate uses of two-way video are developing in institutions with distributed sites. This is a growing phenomenon as pressures to amalgamate institutions and reduce replication of courses increase. Rather than sending teachers to remote sites – some of which may be just across town – videoconferencing is introduced.

Australia is undoubtedly the world leader in the use of ISDN videoconferencing for higher and further education. By mid-1993, 19 of Australia's 35 public universities had videoconferencing facilities at more than 50 sites, and most of the remaining universities were in the process of acquiring them. Uses range from undergraduate lectures and research seminars to small tutorials and specialized presentations. The systems are also heavily used for administrative meetings. Almost all areas of the curriculum are involved. In Australia, videoconferencing is on the same road already travelled by the computer and fax machine.

Thanks to Norwegian Telecom, Norway has been the focus for a variety of small group videoconferencing applications. By involving educators and practitioners in early pilot schemes, and by modifying the technology in response to user feedback, valuable expertise in the educational, psychological and organization aspects of videoconferencing has been gained. Examples include the provision of microphones right in front of students to remove barriers to interaction; the development of competence in making visual material which is legible and appropriate for video presentation; and the use of extra cameras connected to the microphones at remote sites, so that teachers could recognize individual questioners, yet also be able to see the whole group (Klingsheim and Kristiansen, 1993).

International videoconferencing is also on the increase, as costs come down and cross-cultural partnerships develop. These tend to be at the postgraduate and professional level, where buying in an expert is sometimes cheapest by videoconferencing. Training uses of videoconferencing across several countries are also growing, as the equipment is installed for general purpose business activity. The push for ISDN facilities in one country to inter-operate with those in another will support the growth of videoconferencing, especially amongst the various European countries in areas such as language teaching, management and training.

Advantages of videoconferencing

Critics of some videoconferencing applications claim that the technology has been oversold and that there is little demand for visual interactivity in education and training. The unique potential of this medium, therefore, lies in the exploitation of visual communication. The fact that there are very few applications in the area of the visual arts is partly a reflection of current funding priorities, and partly an adherence to traditional lecturing approaches in higher education. Those applications which do involve demonstrations, video inserts or expensive equipment are the exception, and tend to be cited out of all proportion to their occurrence.

However, one important aspect of visual communication lies in the creation of social presence and a comfortable environment for learning. For many learners, a satisfactory level of comfort is only possible with visual contact with the teacher. Those who can exploit the visual aspect of lecturing through their physical presence, voice and manner, and who can adapt to videoconferencing by addressing the camera directly, by reducing gestures and body movement and by acting in a natural and relaxed manner, will contribute to the eventual success of the medium as a positive learning environment.

The ease of interaction through videoconferencing is also an advantage of this medium – compared with computer conferencing and audio-graphics. In small group applications, students can interact with each other across sites in a very natural and spontaneous way. This real-time visual interaction provides a high level of psycho-social support to many types of learners. Although there are small group uses of videoconferencing for administrative interactions, for professional training and postgraduate education, there are many fewer applications at the undergraduate level.

The most often cited advantages of videoconferencing are obviously the reduction in travel time, effort and expense. More significant than these reasons (which are often disputed because the cost, effort and time is simply diverted into other aspects like preparation and support), are the justifications based on doing things which could not be done in any other way. Extending course choice and equal opportunities to rural or remote areas, making scarce expertise available to more people, diverting effort from merely replicating courses at different sites, are examples of these.

Collaborations and partnerships amongst educational institutions are another longer-term benefit of the medium. Separated by distance, these relationships may never have developed before, and they will take time to grow as the medium spreads. Special events and research seminars along with jointly-delivered courses are all beginning to happen using videoconferencing. At the moment, they are more common with educational television:

> Consortia are powerful means to leverage limited resources. They allow a small network to tap into others and eliminate the requirement for the network to oversee all of its own productions. Students are able to select from a wide variety of courses (Pugh *et al.*, 1992).

As with both the other media, the stimulus provided by a new technology provides teachers with new opportunities. For some lecturers, videoconferencing has extended their opportunities for teaching advanced-level courses. For others, the training involved in video lecturing has improved their face-to-face lecturing skills. Partnerships with industry have allowed professionals in the workplace to act as guest or part-time lecturers.

Secondary uses of the equipment provide unexpected advantages with videoconferencing, as with the other two media. One of these is conducting videoconferencing interviews of prospective employees of an educational institution, especially when the interviewee lives abroad.

For students, contact with their peers at other institutions or even in the workplace has been beneficial in widening their perspective on course issues. In those applications which require student presentations, the experience and educational value of preparation and delivery are immense, although students find it very demanding at the time!

The real potential of videoconferencing is often ignored in the haste to make economies or preserve the status quo. Some experienced users of videoconferencing are beginning to acknowledge that it does not make sense to use two-way video to lecture. This should be reserved for one-way video, and small group tutorials should be the model for two-way video. The advent of desktop videoconferencing may also reduce the amount of video lecturing in favour of small group interactions.

Disadvantages of videoconferencing

The cost of videoconferencing equipment and usage charges for higher bandwidth communications links are the major drawbacks at the current time. If a technical facilitator is provided at each site, this will add to the overall costs. All evaluation reports of videoconferencing applications stress the need for a detailed needs analysis, careful costing of the total programme (not just the initial installation costs) and an examination of the relative costs and benefits of other appropriate technologies before committing to videoconferencing. While this medium has been shown to be cost-effective in some contexts, two-way videoconferencing will not be the best solution in many others.

As with audiographics, more preparation time is required by teachers to plan sessions and to make visual material. Most teachers also report that the medium demands much higher energy levels than face-to-face lecturing. The teacher must concentrate simultaneously on the content, the visual material and the students at remote sites. This leads to higher levels of stress during the session and a feeling of exhaustion afterwards. For some teachers the restriction on physical movement during the session also contributes to the level of concentration necessary.

Students also find the medium more intense than face-to-face lectures. The slight blurring of motion and the lack of complete lip synchronization due to compression and slow transmission speeds demand more attention. Some users find that one hour is too long for a videoconferencing session and that frequent pauses or changes of pace are necessary to maintain concentration.

The lack of interactivity in many applications is a cause for some concern – whether students are inhibited by their remoteness from the teacher or intimidated by the video equipment or unaccustomed to taking an active approach to learning. Lecturers must work very hard at encouraging interactivity in the typical videoconferencing size of classes (although this is also the case in large face-to-face lectures). Group dynamics can be difficult to manage in voice-activated systems, where the dominant voice at any site determines which image is transmitted to all sites and the response time is slightly delayed by the slower transmission speed.

Several studies have shown that students prefer the flexibility and asynchronous learning from a recorded video to the benefits of live interaction. This attitude undermines justifications to provide the facility of two-way video and the lecturer's efforts to encourage interactive use. Nevertheless, for the typical videoconference student or trainee – probably a professional with a full-time job and many time pressures – learning must fit in with other commitments. Real-time interactivity may be seen as an expensive luxury. In many respects, this is an attitude engendered by long years of educational practice – examination-oriented, information processing, lecture-dominated teaching. Two-way interaction is not proving to be more effective in the various studies comparing media, because the teaching structure and the measurement concept (final exam results) do not value interaction.

On the whole, the opportunity provided by two-way videoconferencing to alter the way teaching and learning take place has not been seized. More innovative applications and teaching occur with computer conferencing and audiographics than currently with videoconferencing. Lecturing is a perfectly valid, perhaps indispensable, method of conveying, explaining and reinforcing information, but two-way videoconferencing is not necessarily the appropriate medium for it.

Despite the detractors of videoconferencing for education, this is a technology whose power cannot be denied. We live in a visual world, and video images are attractive and compelling. Educators must ultimately harness this medium and put it to good use.

Future trends

Although desktop videoconferencing is available now, its educational exploitation is still in the future. Training applications will undoubtedly be the first to emerge, and it will be some time before developments are student-led rather than technology-driven. Initially the effort to master the abundance of tools available on the desktop will dominate the educational activity.

The synchronous nature of two-way videoconferencing is clearly a drawback for many students – it lacks the flexibility of traditional distance education and the reflective element of computer conferencing. As desktop videoconferencing technology and infrastructures develop, asynchronous forms of education and training may emerge to compensate. Video lectures might be available on demand from the network, just as entertainment videos are now in the USA. Video mail messages to and from the tutor and amongst small groups of students could provide interactivity and collaborative working.

Video on the desktop also extends the range of resources available to the learner as image banks and video sequences in multimedia libraries are accessible over high-speed networks. When video becomes a standard feature on personal computers, software will routinely include video and users will treat it just like any other data. For example, a student could access a training video for a new software package, while at the same time using the program in a separate window. An electronic superhighway to carry this vast amount of data will provide the backbone to make incomparable resources available at the learner's fingertips. Teachers will need a much greater paradigm shift to become guides of the Internet than they have currently made to adapt their lecturing style to accommodate interactivity!

Futurists in the USA talk about the telecomputer, a combination of the visual power of the television and the networking and processing power of the computer. Increasing the bandwidth available in every home, whether by ISDN or optical fibre, is a necessary precursor to 'videoconferencing in the home'.

The growth of networks of all bandwidths is such that government policy towards educational communication will determine the shape of future provision.

> Governments, in consultation with carriers and educational institutions, need to develop policies for educational applications of telecommunications technologies, to provide equity of access, common standards, a unified network strategy that includes all telecommunications services (voice, data, fax, video, etc.) and interconnections both between institutions and with the external world (e.g. with the Internet) (Bates, 1993, p. 8).

In the meantime, the expansion of small group uses of videoconferencing will provide the best experience for the advent of desktop conferencing.

References

Bates, A W (1993) 'Educational aspects of the telecommunications revolution', in Davies, G and Samways, B (eds) *Teleteaching*, Proceedings of the IFIP TC3 Third Teleteaching Conference, Trondheim, Norway, Amsterdam: North-Holland.

Klingsheim, K and Kristiansen, T (1993) 'The importance of user participation in telecommunication', in Davies, G and Samways, B (eds) *Teleteaching*, Proceedings of the IFIP TC3 Third Teleteaching Conference, Trondheim, Norway, Amsterdam: North-Holland.

Pugh, L, Parchman, S and Simpson, H (1992) 'Video telecommunications for distance education: A field survey of systems in US public education, industry and the military', *Distance Education*, **13**, 2.

Chapter 7

Case studies

Rationale

The range of applications of any of these three technologies is much too broad to choose representative examples of usage.

> Researchers and practitioners who seek to maintain some global perspective regarding developments in the use of computer-mediated communication (CMC) may find themselves overwhelmed by the oceanic vastness of the phenomenon. CMC has been implemented with user groups ranging from children to old people, for education and training purposes ranging from psychological counselling to engineering, by organizations ranging from colleges and universities to businesses and local community organizations located on every continent on earth, with the possible exception of Antarctica (Wells, 1993, p. 80).

Although this diversity does not yet apply to either audiographics or videoconferencing, it is difficult to discern with these two newer technologies just what will become the 'typical' application. Cost considerations certainly have a limiting effect – there are few videoconferencing applications in schools, but many in training contexts and in large-scale undergraduate or graduate teaching programmes. Audiographics applications are not nearly as numerous as the other two media, but usage spans all educational and training domains about equally.

The rationale for the nine case studies described here is that they are drawn from different countries and different educational levels and training situations. Each in turn highlights an important or interesting aspect of use which could well be emulated elsewhere, or which might act as inspiration for the reader considering a new application.

Two schools-based case studies are included: Writers in Electronic Residence which is a computer conferencing example from Canada, and MAX, an Australian approach to audiographics in schools.

Two undergraduate-level examples are given: Bestnet, a computer conferencing application with extensions in Africa and Mexico. The other case study involving undergraduates is from Malaysia at a distance education institution using audiographics.

The remaining five case studies involve postgraduate, professional up-dating and training courses. The Online Education and Training course is conducted via computer conferencing and originates from the UK, although its students are worldwide. The videoconferencing example from Northern Ireland involves in-service training for teachers, and the PictureTel videoconferencing application at Columbia University delivers engineering courses (undergraduate and postgraduate) to professional engineers. Two training examples include the use of videoconferencing within France Telecom and a business course using audiographics in Finland.

Each case study is presented in three parts:

- the *context* of the application, which is limited to those details necessary to explain the application;
- the particular *use of the medium*, including concrete examples of course design, implementation of teaching principles and details of how the particular medium was exploited;
- *educational outcomes* of its use, with extracts from evaluation reports and highlights of best practice.

There are three examples for each of the three media:

Medium	*Case Study*
Computer conferencing:	1. Online Education and Training (UK)
	2. Writers in Electronic Residence (Canada)
	3. Bestnet: international computer conferencing (USA)
Audiographics:	4. MAX: audiographics in Victorian schools (Australia)
	5. Audiographics in Malaysia
	6. Multiform education in Tornio (Finland)

Videoconferencing: 7. University of Ulster video-
                                   conferencing (Northern Ireland)
                                   8. ISDN videoconferencing for
                                   engineers (USA)
                                   9. VIF: France Telecom Interactive
                                   Video (France)

1. Online Education and Training

Context

Online Education and Training (OET) is a part-time course at post-graduate level offered jointly by the Institute of Education, University of London and the Institute of Educational Technology, The Open University. In its first two presentations, it was sponsored by the European Commission through its Costel project.

The course is aimed at educationalists and trainers who are interested in using computer conferencing – whether as teachers, network support staff or course designers. Three broad themes are addressed in the course: the effectiveness of online education and collaborative learning; course design using computer conferencing; and online systems and services. The course runs for about 20 weeks and students are expected to spend about 150 hours, either reading the set books or interacting online. About 45–50 students are accepted on each presentation.

The course is run on the Open University conferencing system, CoSy, and is administered by London University (including the award of a certificate upon completion). The tutors for the course include staff from both institutions. Various teaching strategies have been used: one tutor who is responsible for designing and moderating each module of the course, and team teaching with two tutors managing longer modules.

The printed material to accompany the course has also varied from presentation to presentation, as the amount of suitable literature on computer conferencing is extensive. In the first year, offprints of various case studies were used; in subsequent years, two set texts on computer conferencing were used.

Although the course was originally planned for the European market, online advertising has produced an international catchment. The core, however, remains the UK, and this allows two face-to-face meetings to take place. The first is at the beginning of the course for training in the use of CoSy, outlining the course objectives and establishing a social environment for subsequent interactions. The second takes place towards the end of the course, and has in the past given students an opportunity to experience videoconferencing, some by satellite, and others in classrooms of the London University interactive video network, LIVE-NET.

The tutors have always adopted an informal approach to the presentation of the course, by experimenting with different formats in each module (varying the size of groups, the kinds of activities and the type of assessment) and by trying to push the medium to its limits. The aim is to provide students with every opportunity to experience all aspects of the medium.

Use of the medium

The structure of conferences has varied considerably as the tutors search for the optimum arrangement. The pattern of usage so far has been a massive input of messages in the early parts of the course, and a significant tailing off of effort towards the end. These factors require considerable planning and ingenuity to manage.

One of the most successful structures for the beginning of the course was a division of students into three groups, each with their own conference area but with the same discussion question. As a way of allowing for the initial enthusiasm of some students, these areas were not closed to participants in other groups. Students were expected to contribute in their own group, but if they had time and interest and especially if they had no difficulties learning the conferencing system, they could participate in other groups, either by reading the discussion or commenting on the messages. One of the real problems with online courses is that students vary considerably in the time they take to become active and interactive users of the system. Good training and a pre-course period for practising with the system, efficient procedures for getting support materials to students, and sensitive handling by the teacher of the initial conferences, are necessary but not sufficient measures to ensure that students all begin the course together. Late-comers seem to be inevitable and means must be found to help them through the problem of overload and a sense of being left out of the group.

In addition to the three group discussions, a conference was set up in which the tutors (for this month-long module, there were two), summarized the issues being discussed in the three group conferences and highlighted and extended the important points that were being made. Often students were referred to specific messages in the group conferences, so that they could easily find and read a few messages without having to go through the whole conference. Students could also engage in debate with the tutors if they chose, and tutors commented on messages within the three group conferences.

Each week of the module, students were assigned different articles from the set readings and a different focus for discussion. For the assignment at the end of the month, they were asked to upload into a separate conference their choice of five messages from the discussions which best exemplified the cognitive, interactive and social value of computer conferencing; then they had to analyse what made these good examples. Part of the understanding was that other students could read the assignments of their peers.

This structure was only one of a number – others used smaller groups. As this was the first module of the course, it was designed to provide for the needs of the most enthusiastic users as well as the slow and late starters.

Educational outcomes

Although the module just described was well received by students and did not suffer from the main plague of online courses, namely an overload of messages, the course as a whole did have a number of problems.

First of all, some students had a very poor start to the second presentation of the course: late mailings of printed material on how to access the course, inability to obtain the set books, telecommunications and computer difficulties, and upload and download problems, so that they were obliged to work online all the time.

Some students felt that the conferences were dominated by articulate, experienced users with easy and inexpensive access who could enter messages daily. The ten or so second-language students were on the whole less confident and put in far fewer messages.

As for the module one assignment, the tutors intended that students select messages which they themselves had contributed to the discussions. This was to encourage students to become interactive users early on in the course, and not develop the habit of just following passively. However, this caused protest from the students who made very persuasive arguments against the idea and the tutors agreed to widen the range to include any message in the discussion conferences. As various students commented in the conference:

> On the one hand there is all the liberal educational stuff about conferencing being a leveller, encouraging serious discussions and participative learning. But it seems it is usually hard to get this type of discussion. On the other hand, we can fall back on the old 'stick and

carrot' and make the students do it by assessing them. But what is the quality of these assessed messages? They will demonstrate knowledge to assessors rather than making useful points to peers. Do we throw the baby out with the bath water: 'You lot are going to have participative meaningful learning experiences with conferencing, *or else*'.

Computer conferencing seems consciously devised as a group learning mechanism, and should be assessed accordingly. It may well be enough to demonstrate your own learning by showing appreciation of others' contributions.

Although I think the basic idea is a sound one, students experiencing difficulties putting in messages should be able to choose from all messages. It won't solve the problem of lurking, but it might take the pressure off some, and lessen the risk of drop out.

This outcome is a very positive demonstration of the value of computer conferencing as a student-centred medium – students could easily make known their views and these could easily be accommodated. The tutor's role is still vital to the learning process, in structuring and creating an interactive and collaborative environment, but no longer in determining and defining the outcomes. As one student commented in the evaluation of the course:

> I found the course invaluable; the participants themselves explain to a significant extent why this was so, though tutors and organizers 'made' that happen.

2. Writers in Electronic Residence

Context

The Writers in Electronic Residence (WIER) programme connects students in Canada with writers, teachers and one another to discuss and exchange their original writings. The programme began in 1987 with a connection between two schools and has since developed into a national facility with offerings for elementary, middle school and secondary students.

Students use word processors to compose their works and their responses to other works. Their messages are then uploaded to the appropriate conference on the host computer at Simon Fraser University in

Vancouver. Most schools can connect with a local area call, using the Canadian packet-switched service.

Much of the original writing is poetry and short fiction. Students are encouraged to summit works at draft stage in order to benefit from the interactions with the other participants.

Students from Baffin Island in Canada's high Arctic and from urban centres in the south, and first-generation Vietnamese immigrants, Canadian-born Chinese and established Torontonians mix on the system together with a professional writer or poet. The writings reflect this multicultural mix, and although some of the discussion takes place online, much more takes place in the separate classrooms, face-to-face, as teachers draw out the significant elements of this diversity within one country.

The essence of the programme is language-based, and emphasizes the task, not the technology. Students are engaged in a reflective activity which fosters acquisition and use of language for writing and commenting. The uniqueness of the programme lies in the role of the student as reader and critical commentator of other students' work. Sometimes they even comment on original work submitted by the writer-in-electronic-residence. An equally important part of the programme is the students' experience of offering their own work to a wide audience for critical review.

The participation of a recognized Canadian author in each programme has a number of purposes: to de-mystify the concept of books and writers and give students tangible involvement in the writing process. Classroom teachers also benefit from their expertise and external authority.

Use of the medium

The first writer-in-electronic-residence used a range of fake personae in his conferences. These 'students' frequently offered rude remarks about other people's poems and wrote their own terrible poems, which were then attacked by the writer himself.

> The result was a bit of blood letting and a lot of heated and honest discussion about the poems. However, the serious victims were my phantom student personae rather than the actual students, who nevertheless jumped into the fray, and in the process learned a little about how to create literary effects. Seldom have I been able to generate such detached participation in regular face-to-face creative writing workshops (L Kearns, in Owen, 1993).

Revision was a crucial part of the process. The comments from their peers or from the professional writer encouraged students to read over and revise their work. Literary exposure online was much less threatening than in face-to-face situations. Teenagers, particularly, were less self-conscious online and even questioned the opinions of the professional writer.

The practice of evaluating every word in a poem and considering its contribution to the whole was introduced by one of the authors. Nevertheless, she maintained a non-judgemental approach, always emphasizing the primacy of the individual's authority to make revisions or not.

Schools are encouraged to have their students work offline and to download new submissions and responses, and print them out. Students then consider their responses and compose them offline. Messages are thus considered a medium of writing (rather than talking or reacting). This produces a kind of interaction which is conversational and informal in tone, yet is the product of reflection and careful preparation.

The final element in the programme is the use of the online material as a vehicle for extending students' experience and understanding of issues outside their normal environment. Stories written by children from very different backgrounds, poems expressing personal experiences and images then become subjects of study alongside Shakespeare and Wordsworth.

> It never occurred to me that you could be a poet and be Canadian at the same time. Things worth writing about happened some place else – in London, Paris, maybe Toronto, but never in Swift Current, Saskatchewan. And things worth writing about happened to other people (L Crozier, in Owen, 1993).

Educational outcomes

One of the most significant outcomes of this programme is the legitimization of students' original writing as reading material in the classroom. This came about through the interactions with professional authors, who encouraged students to see that their own experience and their skill in conveying it was the stuff of writing.

Evaluation reports indicate that students' writing had improved but, even more significantly, students demonstrated a greater investment in their own learning.

Teachers also received considerable support from the programme. When the professional writer or other students made the same comments on a student's work as the classroom teacher, this increased their credibility. Some teachers reported that they had changed their teaching in response to the nature of the conferencing interactions where the focus of all comments was the writing, not the student. These teachers altered their own practices so that they spent more time responding to the writing – with the student – and less time giving marks or marking work in isolation.

The text-based nature of the communication was considered ideal for the programme. Its asynchronicity encouraged reflection and considered response. It also fitted in with school timetables spanning many time zones. The use of written language both for original work and for criticism and comment made a major contribution to the development of language and communication skills.

The relative anonymity of the medium helped students to develop the necessary attitude of detachment and objectivity towards their own writing.

> If a young writer does not take that chance of exposing the work to the critical gaze of others, he or she will never learn how to write something that moves a reader (L Kearns, in Owen, 1993).

The contact with students outside the classroom walls also contributed to the success of the programme. The task of responding to students' writing focused the student-to-student interactions on content and created a vehicle for a real exchange of experiences and perspectives. (This case study was based on a report by Trevor Owen, 1993).

3. Bestnet: international computer conferencing

Context

'Bestnet' stands for the Binational English–Spanish Telecommunications Network, and is an international consortium of institutions of higher education, sponsored in part by Digital Equipment Corporation. Four of the collaborating institutions are in the southern United States and two are in Mexico. There are also associate institutions and, most recently, Bestnet has been extended to involve universities in Kenya and Zimbabwe. The Bestnet model is based on a series of interconnected nodes so that the user need only log onto the local node and interconnections are automatically made to conferences and databases on distant nodes. With this kind of distributed network, there is no centre. The system operates on a basis of a shared sense of responsibility and an attitude of mutual benefit.

The particular use of computer conferencing described in this case study involves San Diego State University only. (As the international and particularly African connections are still being established, case study material of courses is not yet available.) The context for the application centered on a major problem faced by the University: the need to provide more flexible scheduling of courses as the typical undergraduate student is now over 25 and works at least part-time.

Consequently, for one particular course, conventional class meetings were replaced by computer communication, videocassettes, and print, thus freeing students to take the course on their own weekly schedule. Students were not obliged to own special equipment to take the course, as all facilities were available on campus. However, those who had a computer, modem and telephone could access the conferencing system from home, and those with a television and a VCR could buy the videocassettes.

The course transferred to this new delivery mode was entitled 'Technological Trends in Telecommunication', for upper division and graduate students in the Department of Telecommunications and Film.

The intention was to produce a low-budget, easily replicable course by using existing facilities and software, and by making real-time videos with minimal editing and no special effects. Sixteen hours of video were pre-recorded with a format consisting either of a lecture with professionally produced graphics or interviews with guest experts in various areas of telecommunications.

Use of the medium

The emphasis for the use of computer conferencing was on student participation and the notion that all participants could read the contributions of their peers. The principal conferences for the course were:

- TechNews, to which students contributed weekly an abstract of an article from current publications concerning telecommunications or information technology. The conference was organized by categories of technology, so that as the semester progressed the students were creating a database of current developments in technology;
- InfoWeek, in which students responded weekly to issues posed by the professor. The issues were keyed to the videos and reading assignments of the course;
- Seminar, for the sharing of term papers;
- Groupthink, in which students entered and commented upon collaborative research projects. Each student belonged to one group;
- Telepub, a meeting place for discussions on any topic;

- CourseInfo, a repository for information about the course itself; for example, the course calendar and syllabus.

Two guest lecturers were also available online, one of whom had also been a guest on video. Students appreciated most being able to interact with the guest whom they had seen on the course video.

One element of the course involved formal collaboration. Each student was assigned to work in one of ten groups to produce a collaborative paper. The grade of the paper would be assigned to each of the group's members. A conference was created for each of the groups to use as a discussion space.

The course included a set of tasks for each week of the semester as a way of helping students to pace themselves. Grades were based on the quality of work in the weekly assignments, the longer writing assignments, the group research, and a series of open-book essay exams related to the reading assignments and videos.

Forty students enrolled the first time the course was offered in the fall semester, 1991. Several surveys were carried out to assess students' reactions to the course. Some face-to-face interviews were also conducted.

Educational outcomes

By nearly three to one, students agreed that the professor was more accessible than is normally the case in a traditional class structure. While most students would prefer to interact face-to-face, the majority felt that this course offered more personalized attention from the instructor than normal courses do. Furthermore, by nearly two to one, students agreed that the format of the course allowed them to learn from other students in a way that traditional courses do not. The majority also said that the online format enhanced their learning. Of the students who felt that a traditional class setting does not provide an enviroment wherein they feel comfortable expressing themselves, all believed that this online format was an improvement.

One survey investigated the degree of collaboration which took place on the course. Three quarters of the survey respondents indicated that group members coordinated their efforts and that the final product was a genuinely collaborative effort. However, at least three groups felt that they had one member who did not participate effectively. The extent to which the computer conferencing system was used in the collaborative work varied considerably. Most groups in fact used face-to-face meetings to facilitate collaboration. Some used the telephone and one group used fax. Email and conferencing were used to coordinate group meetings, but only one group used conferencing extensively as the primary means of working together. Significantly, most members of this group had computers and modems at home or work. They reported that the major advantage was that each member's work was accessible to the others, and they shared research sources and tips and kept up with each other's progress.

Feedback from students generally indicated that home access to the conferencing system would make a major improvement to the format. The computer labs on campus were considered unpleasant places to spend time.

The professor who taught the course observed immediately that the students' writing was better than in the previous conventional offering of the course, and that their online responses were longer and more detailed than anticipated. Based on the quality of written work and the sophistication of questions raised in interactions, he concluded that the online course format resulted in a higher standard of learning. One of the reasons for this was that students greatly valued the facility to read the work of their colleagues and the knowledge that other students would read their work acted as a positive motivating force.

A significant drawback, however, is that this format takes substantially more time to teach effectively than a conventional lecture and discussion course. The time involved in producing videos can be amortized over a few semesters, but the online interaction is a significant daily commitment. The professor concludes, nevertheless:

> Teaching the course in this way is an enormously satisfying experience. It is also a major personal and professional commitment. If heavy-duty academic Calvinism can be fun, this is it (Witherspoon *et al.*, 1992).

4. MAX: audiographics in Victorian schools

Context

The Department of School Education in Victoria, Australia, embarked on an audiographics programme to improve the retention rate of students attending rural schools as long ago as 1986. In telecommunications applications, this is a venerable history! By bringing rural schools together into clusters to share resources and teaching expertise, a broader curriculum with live interactive support could be offered to students to encourage them to stay on at school after the statutory school-leaving age. Teachers were invited to draw up a list of educational requirements for the technology to be chosen. They asked for the following:

- an audio link for voice contact;
- a document link to send both handwritten and typed material;
- a blackboard facility for exchange of graphics, drawings or other writing arising from live interactions.

What developed from these requirements was a system consisting of Macintosh computers with audiographics software, FAX machines and an audio system. Called Mac/Fax/Audio, it was soon abbreviated to MAX. The software developer has, for each modification or update, involved the teachers in design and field trials, so that the system has continued to grow from their needs.

Over 200 sites use the MAX system, with anywhere up to six locations simultaneously linked in to the *Electronic Classroom*. When not used for networking classes, the equipment can be separated and used in stand-alone mode for either teaching, administration or course preparation. Staff development and discussion amongst schools in the same cluster also take place using the system. Furthermore, through parents, the local community has become aware of the potential of the system for adult education and other services.

The system is not only versatile but it accommodates a variety of teaching styles. Many teachers began with the audio and FAX equipment, and moved on gradually to include the audiographics capability once they were more confident of their skills. As confidence and experience grow, various peripherals can be added to extend the scope of the programme: a large monitor can be added to work with bigger groups; a printer allows paper copies of work to be made and a scanner allows users to input material not prepared on computer.

Use of the medium

The teacher initiates a class by clicking the names of the appropriate schools on a menu – dialling and connection are automatic. Teachers may draw freehand on the screen using either a mouse or a pen; built-in tools for making lines, rectangles or circles are also available. Pre-prepared graphics or text can be accessed and brought up on all the linked screens. Some teachers plan a whole lesson of material and prepare screens beforehand; others use a more responsive style and react to student-initiated contributions.

The teacher controls the turn-taking, but can pass control to another school so that students at remote sites can draw or type on the shared screen. New screens can be created at any time, and old screens can be stored, printed out or re-used by the teacher at subsequent sessions. Students can also prepare material and share it with other sites during the class.

One of the curriculum areas most appropriate for MAX is second-language learning – because rural schools find it difficult to offer these courses, and audiographics provides good support for language practice with peers and with teachers.

Mathematics is another area in which MAX has been especially valuable:

> It was found that when individual guidance with mathematics problems is withheld by a teacher within the classroom, some students tend to give up easily. However, when working through the same problem using the computer as an electronic blackboard and with only an audio link, the students at the other sites tend to forget that the teacher is watching and listening at the other end and proceed to work through the problem independently. Also, in such a situation, the visual link and audio system provide a 'window into the students' minds' and the remote teacher is often actually better placed to follow the students' mental reasoning than when they are physically present in the room (Conboy, 1993, p. 191).

As use of MAX has grown, the cluster form of school organization has also grown. First of all, schools within a cluster have standardized their timetables and, using MAX, have run coordination committee meetings to agree curriculum provision and determine which courses can be given from within the cluster and which will need resources from other clusters. Some clusters have begun to offer their MAX facilities to local higher education institutions and become study centres for adult literacy and return-to-study courses within the community.

Educational outcomes

Evaluation reports on the MAX programme conclude that its outstanding success is based on the simultaneous top-down and bottom-up approach. The programme was initiated at state level, but unlike many state-funded projects, it did not begin with tentative pilots trials and small contained experiments. About 20 per cent of Victoria's schools were identified as potential users and A\$3.5m was allocated for the project. At the same time, teachers were involved in key decision-making processes and provided with a two-day training workshop if they chose to use the system. Retaining individual school autonomy has continued to be an important element in the use of the system, as has the flexibility for teachers to develop their own teaching strategies.

The major benefit for students has been the interactivity with the teacher and their peers at other schools. Previously, students had to take advanced courses via correspondence, and work largely on their own with very delayed feedback from the teacher. Evaluation studies report that MAX-delivered courses lead to improved quality and depth of learning. The challenge and stimulation of contact with a larger peer group has made the major contribution to this result. Access to a wider curriculum choice has also contributed to the rise in the number of students staying on at school.

In addition to the original goal of improving student retention rates, MAX has provided a significant learning process for the teachers themselves. Many have been introduced to the use of computers through their experience with MAX. Interaction with teachers at other schools has also been beneficial, as has the opportunity to teach new subjects or more senior students. Some teachers have commented on how the lack of direct visual contact with students has improved their listening and communication skills. All the teachers agree that teaching via audiographics requires more preparation time than traditional teaching, but most see this as beneficial to their teaching. Various staff development activities – some initiated at state level, and some arising spontaneously through cluster discussions – have added to the benefits of the medium. Teacher loyalty to the programme has grown from their sense of ownership of it.

The MAX system has had a major impact on rural education in Victoria. Those responsible for planning and introducing the system have had to focus on what is acceptable within the context of rural schools and what is practicable within the typical classroom.

> However, it may be in the second-order consequences that the project has had its biggest impact. The project has increased communication among schools, given rise to new forms of cooperation and empowered teachers and communities to engage in new self-help enterprises (Conboy, 1993, p. 197).

Second-order consequences turning into the most significant outcomes is not uncommon with telecommunications applications. This is undoubtedly because communication is an agent of change, and electronic communication opens up channels of flow and creates new patterns with unexpected outcomes. (I am indebted to Ian Conboy for his excellent report on MAX, and refer the reader to his bibliography for further evaluations of this application; Conboy, I, 1993).

5. Audiographics in Malaysia

Context

The Centre for Off-Campus Studies of the University of Sains Malaysia was established in 1971 and is the country's only tertiary distance education institution. Its aim is to offer a full degree programme to adults who have missed the opportunity for higher education. Although students take the last quarter of their degree on campus as full-time students, the rest of their courses consist primarily of self-instructional printed materials studied at a distance.

In 1987, the centre introduced audioconferences as a means of supporting distance students. These replaced face-to-face tutorials held at regional centres by tutors hired locally. The centre had found difficulties in employing reliable tutors in certain locations and especially so for high-level courses. Tutors were also considered ineffective, for example at elaborating difficult concepts, and some lacked dedication and professionalism. Audioconferences were run by the lecturers at the centre who had designed and written the courses. This direct contact between lecturer and students enabled greater equity in support to all students and allowed the lecturer to check progress and help any student falling behind.

An electronic writing board was incorporated with the audioconferencing system in 1989, and consisted of a writing pad which displayed handwritten characters or graphics. A built-in floppy disk drive in the control unit enables playback of the data. The cost of installing equipment in regional centres and using central academics to tutor the courses is much less than employing part-time tutors.

One of the aims of the distance education programme is to develop self-directed learners, defined as:

> the ability to effectively cope with pressure and stress that accompanies academic work and other aspects of living and the knowledge to seek out, identify and utilise every available resource in carrying out their learning activities and in evaluating their progress towards their objectives (Idrus, 1992a, p. 52).

To encourage this active learning approach, the audiographics tutorials have on some courses been designed for collaborative work amongst students in each regional centre. Lecturers on the early audioconferences noticed the extreme reluctance of some students to participate. Collaborative work is seen as a way of counteracting traditional Malaysian hierarchical attitudes towards the teacher.

Use of the medium

The collaborative learning sessions work in two phases. Students attend their nearest regional centre for discussions with their fellow students one hour before the audiographics session begins. Each student has done their own study of the printed materials and uses this hour for:

- discussion of the basics of the topic;
- sorting out any simple problems or misunderstandings;
- explanations of the material by the stronger students to the weaker ones;
- collective decisions on a pool of questions to put to the plenary session.

The second phase is the actual audiographics session with the lecturer and the students at other regional centres. This is student-led as each site has its own set of collaboratively agreed questions. The lecturer facilitates discussion of these questions in a spirit of mutual inquiry. The electronic writing board is an effective medium for handling inquiry as students sometimes have difficulty expressing their question purely verbally, and the teacher uses the board to make explanations more visual and hence concrete.

This collaborative learning process is currently used on the science foundation programme, and it is reinforced during the three-week annual residential school. Students meet to work out a collective set of problems before the tutorial session begins.

Experience of running teletutorials has convinced the centre of the importance of sending out supporting materials to students before the session.

The question of class size for these tutorials is the subject of some debate. Some lecturers feel that sessions can only be really interactive with small student numbers. Others find that with very thorough planning, large classes can still be interactive.

The use of lecturers and audiographics rather than local tutors means much higher demands on central academics. Furthermore, they are obliged to run these sessions during weekends. This is the only realistic choice, as students have to travel as much as 150km to attend regional offices. Each course is allocated between two and eight of these one-hour teleconferences per year.

Educational outcomes

The primary educational outcome of the switch to audiographics has been in the direct contact between students and the lecturer in charge of the off-campus course. The lecturer is best placed to initiate and supervise a programme of self-directed learning. All the facilities provided are directed towards encouraging the teacher-dependent Malaysian students to organize and take responsibility for their own learning. This is seen as a very major departure from the traditional approach and will take time to have an effect. In the short term, the new communications and instructional technologies gave students the opportunity to develop a wider range of learning skills and to overcome the isolation of print-based distance learning.

The introduction of audiographics had a number of limitations as well as some advantages. The major problem in this Malaysian application was breakdown in the transmission lines (about 1.4 per cent). Although not high, it has a demoralizing effect on all concerned. Secondly, lecturers and students alike found that audiographics tutorials are tiring and demanding. On the other hand, the interactivity of the system, in conjunction with the collaborative strategy, helped to overcome the Malaysian concept of learning as a private activity.

As with many distance education students, Malaysians find that part-time study usually means giving up friendships, activities or hobbies for which there is no longer enough time. One secondary value of the student-to-student collaborative sessions is that they counteract these changes in lifestyle:

> Course-mates become new friends and the quest for knowledge and the interaction during study become the new activities and social interaction (Indrus, 1992b).

Audiographics supports the model of a social environment for learning.

The audiographic system is also used for meetings between lecturers and administrators at the centre and staff at the regional offices. In addition, public workshops and seminars are held via teleconference. (Details for this case study come from three papers: Idrus, 1992a, 1992b; and Nordin, 1992.)

6. Multiform education in Tornio

Context

Tornio in northern Finland is one of the five areas chosen to carry out development projects in the country's adult education policy called 'multiform education'. The Kemi-Tornio Polytechnic has begun an open and flexible education programme which consists of three parts: face-to-face sessions, distance education (using a range of media) and integration with the workplace. The students are adults living in very remote areas of Lapland and working during the daytime, so that they have very few options for continuing their education after formal schooling. The multiform programme aims to meet these students' needs by fitting education around their other committments, while at the same time integrating it with their on-the-job problems.

All three elements of the multiform programme are conceived as one whole, whereby the social contact offered by the face-to-face sessions nurtures the interactions at a distance, and the problems encountered at work can be discussed by the group in the evening sessions. In addition, students are encouraged to pass on the skills acquired during the course to their fellow workmates, so that a cascade effect will be felt in these remote regions.

The telecommunications media used to the greatest extent have been electronic mail, audioconferencing and audiographics. Electronic mail is used by the teachers to send questions and exercises to students, and for students to exchange ideas and solutions with each other.

In 1986, audioconferencing was introduced for distance teaching and the teachers had some reticence about using it, as they had no experience of technology-mediated distance education. Initially they would prepare a written lecture to deliver over the telephone. With more experience they began to rely on the interactions of the students to make the sessions lively and engaging. When audiographics became available in 1991, the teachers had some experience on which to build for developing appropriate courses. Although both media continue to be used, audiographics is seen as having the greatest potential for further growth.

Using a mix of media is intended to add flexibility to the course as well as to cater for different learning styles. Students are encouraged to support each other outside the teaching sessions, and to work on problems and activities together.

Use of the medium

In September 1992, a further education course in computer science was started at the Tornio Institute of Business and Data Processing. Computer applications, such as word processing and spread sheets, and book keeping, accounting and wage programs are the main contents of the course.

The students come from different parts of the province of Lapland and are spread 300 kilometres apart. The 14 students on the course are aged between 25 and 40, and have different employment backgrounds: tourism, health care, construction and banking.

At five-week intervals, the students have face-to-face seminar days, where the teacher gives an introduction to the material to be studied during the following distance learning period. Audiographics sessions take place on several nights each week. These are supplemented by audioconferences and electronic mail. The course takes three semesters and finishes in January 1994. In all, 912 lessons will have taken place, of which about half are through audiographics (using a system called VIS-A-VIS).

Most of the students meet in groups of two to four for the audiographics sessions, but one student, located in the most northerly area outside Muonio, is on her own. Because this multiform education programme has the financial support of the Finnish National Board of Education, the Tornio Institute is able to provide the audiographics equipment to students for the duration of the course. In two cases, students use the equipment in their own home (and have received funds to install a second telephone line).

A typical audiographics session consists of a discussion of the activities previously sent to students via email, as well as explanations from the teacher. Although the whole session may last for two hours, the telephone connection may be broken off at several points during this time in order that students can work through a task. When the connection is resumed, students present their solutions and discuss them with other groups.

At various points the teacher might scan in a program code for the other sites to consider. Students also bring problems from their workplace for discussion amongst the group or for advice from the teacher.

Occasionally the telephone connection is interrupted at one or more sites. As long as the graphics link is not broken as well, it is easy for the student to simply write a message on the screen, and the teacher can then redial that site.

Educational outcomes

Feedback from students on the course indicates that they are very positive about this programme. Like the teachers on the course, they are highly motivated and interested in using new methods. Certainly there is a strong preference for audiographics, rather than audioconferencing. Not surprisingly, these students do better with this programme than those who study face-to-face. The lack of other educational alternatives gives these students a strong incentive.

The interaction amongst students has been one of the most significant advantages of the use of audiographics. The teacher noted how animated and interactive the sessions became when he took a coffee break, and this collaborative activity soon dominated much of the work.

The face-to-face sessions were important, not for pedagogical reasons – the students felt that any material could be taught via audiographics – but for the social/psychological benefits. The students definitely found the face-to-face sessions the best part of the course. They provided the foundation upon which the interactions during the periods of distance education were based.

The organizational implications of the use of audiographics involve the provision of technical support. Teachers need to have technical back-up particularly in the initial stages of using the system. The Tornio Institute also provides help in the preparation of graphical material.

The value of audiographics in this application, and many others, is that it uses ordinary telephone lines. In a sparsely populated area like Lapland, where the public telephone company is not investing in a digital network, audiographics is a low-cost solution to interactive distance education.

Although this course has been experimental, there is considerable interest in expanding the use of audiographics and in establishing a network of sites with the appropriate equipment. The idea of study centres where students could go to take courses from any educational institution in Finland is very appealing. Indeed, this network could be connected to similar networks throughout Europe. With this model, the equipment is owned by the study centre and not by the distance teaching institution. (My thanks to Juha Merilinen, Markku Henriksson, Outi Ponkala and Eero Pekkarinen of the Tornio Institute of Business and Data Processing for their assistance in providing information for this case study.)

7. University of Ulster videoconferencing

Context

This case study is exceptional in its use of videoconferencing for small group, highly interactive seminars. Furthermore, in the particular instance described here, all the students were at one site and the tutor was alone at the other. It therefore presents quite different advantages and limitations from the large-scale, lecture-mode courses used in the majority of videoconferencing applications.

The University of Ulster, in common with many tertiary education institutions, is a distributed campus with sites in cities many kilometres apart. During the 1980s, experiments were made with audioconferencing as a way of linking postgraduate students on two campuses. Although students benefited from the audio communications, they did not recommend its continuation.

From 1990, videoconferencing has been used on several sites in order to gather enough students to make certain postgraduate courses viable. Participants and evaluators of this programme feel strongly that videoconferencing should be seen as a form of open and distance education, not as a substitute for face-to-face teaching.

The equipment used is a relatively inexpensive videoconferencing system marketed by BT (formerly British Telecom). Three cameras are used:

- the first is focused on the student group and can be robotically controlled to zoom in on any student making a sustained contribution;
- the second is located at the back of the room and is focused on the tutor, who can manually control its movement;
- the third is placed above a rostrum for showing the graphic material.

The use of the robotic camera led to a fixed seating pattern of chairs in rows, which constrained the development of an informal small group discussion atmosphere. Similarly, the ceiling microphones did not pick up the discussion of small groups working together at the distant site, so the tutor was unable to drop in on their interactions.

Some classes – such as the first two – were held face-to-face in order to develop a group rapport. The evaluators of the programme consider it essential for the tutor to meet with the students in person, and for the numbers of students to be kept below 12.

Use of the medium

The most significant aspect of this application of the medium was that it involved discussion of very sensitive subject matter – education for mutual understanding, in which ways of improving relationships between people of different cultural traditions were studied by teachers, themselves representing the two traditions in Northern Ireland.

All eight of the students who enrolled for the courses in 1991/2 were at one site while the tutors were at another. This meant that tutors had to devise strategies for facilitating group work at a distance.

The classes generally included a short time devoted to a presentation by the tutor, a period of group work, and a discussion period between the tutor and students. One course also included student presentations in which the student was responsible for presenting the topic, operating the robotic or rostrum cameras and chairing the ensuing discussion. The content of full lectures was delivered to students by post, so that one-way tutor presentations were minimized.

Nevertheless, tutors reported that teaching via videoconference definitely increased their preparation time. Generally they welcomed the opportunity to plan their sessions a week in advance, so that students knew exactly what to do, and no videoconferencing time was wasted on organizational matters.

After approximately one hour, a break was made in the videoconferencing link to counteract the effects of 'techno-stress'. Concentration is much more intense in technology-mediated classes, and attention spans are therefore shortened. With this videoconferencing equipment, windows had to be kept shut to exclude extraneous noise, and bright lights were necessary to improve picture quality.

During the periods of group work, the tutor was available over the videoconferencing link, but the students organized their work independently, discussing and sharing out elements of the task. Sometimes this involved simulation exercises, role play sessions or preparation of a joint report.

Because of regular maintenance work, one class was delivered by audioconferencing only. Although this allowed students to sit around the audio unit, rather than in formal rows, and even though the sound quality was better than that for videoconferencing, the students were not nearly as satisfied with the session. One student commented that the loss of visual contact gave an impersonal feeling, and that listening lacked stimulation, after they had become accustomed to visual input. The tutor found the discussion of sensitive and potentially divisive issues more difficult to negotiate without visual cues.

Educational outcomes

The group cohesiveness which developed from this small group application was its most positive outcome. Independent group learning improved in quality and pace as the course progressed, according to both students and tutors:

> Guidance was given on appropriate reports and other literature, and they were able, in many cases, to access further documentation in the form of discipline policies or working papers from their own schools. . ... They undertook the writing of separate parts of the element, assembled and edited it, and finalised it in agreed form. Not only did they achieve their common goal, but they felt the groupwork involved to be one of the most successful parts of the module (Abbott *et al.*, 1993, p. 56).

The students felt that eight was the optimum group size for developing the cohesion and independence to work together effectively. The physical absence of the tutor helped them to focus on and evaluate their own experiences, and to feel less inhibited in expressing their own views and feelings.

With the student-led seminars, both tutors reported that they would have liked more free-flowing discussion with, for instance, students taking on the task of guiding and initiating the topic. Most students prepared too much material and left little time for discussion. Having to manipulate the videoconferencing equipment was daunting to some students, and the graphics they displayed were not always legible.

Student evaluations show a high level of satisfaction with tutor organization and preparation. Receiving material a week in advance meant that students could prepare for the class and feel comfortable about what would be expected of them during class time. The positive group dynamics which characterized the courses emanated partially from this state of preparedness.

Conclusions about the use of videoconferencing by the evaluators include the following:

- the advantages of using videoconferencing for teaching and learning are pragmatic rather than pedagogical (that is, videoconferencing solves the practical problem of distance);
- the use of videoconferencing affects styles of teaching more than styles of student learning; videoconferencing challenges the tutor more than the learner;
- the use of videoconferencing might not reduce the content of the course but it can hold back the contribution of students and thereby place more onus on the tutor. (For further details of the videoconferencing applications at the University of Ulster, see Abbott *et al.*, 1993.)

8. ISDN videoconferencing for engineers

Context

Columbia University's graduate-level distance learning programme began in 1986 with a system of dedicated high-speed lines, which allowed only fixed point-to-point video communications. Since then the programme has migrated to a digital compressed video system which offers multi-point connectivity over two 56 kbit/s telephone lines. Most local exchange carriers in the United States now offer this service, known as 'Switched 56'. This system is far more versatile than the fixed lines, and is much cheaper — costs are charged according to time used, at about twice the amount of a standard telephone call.

The Off-Campus Graduate Education Program serves the needs of engineering professionals by providing graduate degree programmes in several engineering disciplines. This programme is based on partnership with industry, and students are supported by their employees both financially and administratively.

Courses transmitted by Columbia are held in specially equipped video classrooms. Computer output can be fed into the system, as well as video clips, the usual graphics and blackboard lecturing material. Unlike other applications, Columbia employs undergraduate students to control cameras and audio systems remotely from control rooms adjacent to the classrooms. Consequently, the lecturer is free to concentrate on the material and the students.

Most off-campus receiving sites are also purpose-built videoconferencing rooms with a conference table for eight to twelve students. As these facilities are also used for other meetings and events, conflicts sometimes occur in which training has to give way to upper management priorities. Mobile or rollabout systems are therefore recommended for most corporate sites, so that room allocations can be made according to numbers each semester.

All courses are taught live to on-campus students and simultaneously transmitted to remote sites. Some off-campus students take the courses through tutored videotape instruction, in which a tape of the class is received the next morning, and students view it with their local group and a tutor or facilitator who leads local discussion.

Express mail, fax and electronic mail are all used for handouts and written assignments. Peer learning groups exist amongst on-campus and off-campus students, some of whom use electronic communication.

Use of the medium

Several class formats are used by the 100 or so lecturers who have taught via videoconferencing at Columbia. Senior faculty with an established reputation in the field tend to use traditional lecture methods. These include minimal hand-out material, blackboard lecturing and weekly assignments. Notetaking is essential for students. Interaction is limited to the beginning of the lecture in which students may ask questions concerning the previous assignment.

However, lectures from experts have a number of advantages: they are generally well composed and cogent at the same time as they are stimulating and approachable. Often they involve the very latest research, and with the support of technical staff can include videos of recent laboratory activities, experiments and demonstrations. Lecturers review and comment on all student work, although teaching assistants are employed to assist this process.

Other lecturers use a much more interactive or pre-prepared approach. For example, some lecturers engage remote students in discussions involving their experience as professional engineers with real-world issues and problems of industry. Sometimes this kind of lecturer will leave the podium and join students in a discussion circle. Sound and image are controlled by the technician from the control room. Students may have a portion of their grades dependent on their participation. Student presentations are often required, and those taking the course by videotape rather than live, can make their presentation by submitting a videotape.

Some lecturers provide a course guide including notes and graphs at the beginning of the semester. This gives a list of activities and time scales for the course and is available to both on-campus and off-campus students.

Prospective lecturers are offered considerable training and on-going support from the Columbia Video Network Program. They receive a presentation and booklet on the dos and don'ts of lecturing via videoconferencing, along with an opportunity to practise the concepts and tactics by being videotaped for immediate review and feedback. Furthermore, staff are available to assist lecturers with the preparation and delivery of printed material, to make in-house videos of demonstrations or to adapt existing video material.

Finally, faculty on the programme receive an extra payment above base salary for the additional effort of teaching via videoconferencing. This includes a flat fee to compensate for the preparation of lectures and material. Both faculty and teaching assistants also receive an amount for each student enrolled in the course by video, in consideration of the extra effort involved in serving off-campus students.

Educational outcomes

Columbia originally chose videoconferencing because it most resembled face-to-face instruction and required the least change in traditional teaching methods. As the programme has evolved, so has a new approach to distance learning. Quality is no longer measured by similarity to conventional classroom experience. In fact, both face-to-face and distance education have been enhanced by the advantages and constraints of videoconferencing. For example:

- the need for well-prepared graphical material, legible writing and clear speech on videoconferencing has encouraged lecturers to improve their delivery in all aspects of their teaching;
- the presence of an on-campus class is important to the lecturer and to those taking the course via videotape, because they provide the instructor with feedback and questions;
- on-campus students benefit from interaction with off-campus students who have direct experience of working in the field;
- both on-campus and off-campus students have access to a videotape of the classes as a back-up, in case a scheduling conflict arises or for review purposes. Many students value this flexibility.

Students report that the most significant element in the success of a course is not the medium but a clearly communicated course plan, and some form of student/instructor interaction. This need not necessarily be synchronous, and increasing use is being made of electronic mail and other supporting technologies, such as audioconferencing.

The benefits of the programme for Columbia include the extra income from students who would not be able to attend in any other way. However, more long-term advantages are also perceived from this partnership with industry: increased opportunities for faculty to consult and develop research relationships with industry, and opportunites to develop new courses, often with industry support.

The main benefit to the industrial partners in the programme lies in their access to excellent academic programmes provided to their staff without loss of time and energy in travel. Secondary benefits include the increased opportunities for their leading scientists and engineers to serve as adjunct faculty, and their employees' practice in applying what is learned to problems and opportunities at work. (This case study is derived from Borbely, 1993.)

9. VIF: France Telecom Interactive Video

Context

France Telecom uses its in-house videoconferencing system, VIF, to deliver training to all kinds of its personnel: technical, design, management and sales. VIF has a unique system involving high quality live satellite broadcasting for transmitting visual training material, combined with interactive video returns via CODECs and ISDN from remote sites.

The medium offers the following advantages: training can be more integrated, coordinated and more responsive to the needs of trainees. First of all, using videoconferencing (rather than face-to-face or print-based training) reduces the delivery time for training programmes. At the same time, it makes training more consistent across the whole company. These are significant factors for a company of several thousand staff spread over a wide geographical area, which includes all of France and Corsica, Guyana and the island of Reunion.

The VIF system includes two types of receive sites: 45 *Centre Local Interactif* (CLI) which support two-way interactive audio and video, and many more *Centre Local Recepteur* (CLR) which support one-way video with feedback via telephone, videotex or FAX. The training is broadcast from a central production studio, *Centre Directeur* (CD), where the trainers and video production team are located. Five CLI sites can participate simultaneously, and any number of CLR sites.

The VIF system is essentially a managed service; that is, the view received on the monitors at the remote sites is controlled and selected by the director from the centre. This centre is equipped and run like a television studio; there is no studio audience. The trainers sit or stand on a set under studio lights. The planning and delivery of the training is carried out by a professional production team, consisting of a project manager who is in charge of the training programme, the trainers themselves, a broadcast director, his assistant, camera operators, graphic artists, various craftsmen and signal and sound technicians. The broadcast is directed from a control room, where the director views a bank of monitors and chooses which image to send to all sites (see Figure 7.1).

VIF allows much more flexibility in the management of training. For example, if additional staff register their interest half-way through a series of training broadcasts, additional sessions can easily be run to respond to demand.

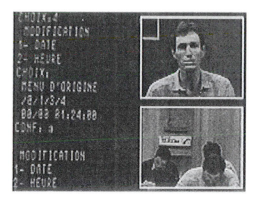

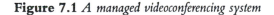

Photos courtesy of VIF

Figure 7.1 *A managed videoconferencing system*

Use of the medium

The training sessions vary considerably in length, content and structure. Between 50 and 100 trainees is typical for any one training programme, and day-long sessions are the most common. The range of content includes the demonstration and use of specialized equipment, changes and upgrading of telecommunications procedures, and product information before a sales launch.

The VIF system is, of course, also used for a wider coordination function within France Telecom. For example, special interest groups use videoconferencing to keep abreast of the latest developments; special broadcasts in which senior management disseminate policy and ethos throughout the company, are another use. Altogether, training accounts for 38 per cent of the system usage, and this wider coordinating function the other 62 per cent.

VIF sessions are highly structured. The ratio of presentation to interaction is usually 50:50. Lectures or presentations of information are interspersed with more interactive question and answer periods, although not open-ended discussion. Demonstrations followed by a guided exploration of a piece of equipment are common. VIF sessions have explicit objectives and a pre-prepared route to achieving them. Each must adhere to an agreed script and the schedule for the day.

Most sessions include pre-prepared graphics, computer inputs, music or video inserts, as well as live interactions and demonstrations. The director in the control studio not only selects an image to broadcast, but also can combine images, such as both trainer and trainee asking a question, speaker and equipment, or speaker and a list of instructions (see Figure 7.2). In short, the VIF system is not conceived as an imitation of face-to-face sessions; it was designed to use the full technological possibilities of videoconferencing. The result is a highly polished, professional look to the sessions.

Photos courtesy of VIF

Figure 7.2 *Creating visual interest in a 'managed' system*

VIF sessions also make good use of key specialists, such as experts on a particular issue or a new piece of equipment. By participating in training by videoconferencing, their expertise can be shared amongst many more trainees than would be economical with face-to-face training. Trainees are said to be more confident of, and more satisfied with, the information they acquire during training, if they believe that it is provided by the most authoritative source.

Some training programmes make use of interaction between sites, for example, trainees from different areas comparing and contrasting their experience of a piece of equipment.

Educational outcomes

Frequent, short, timely courses with a high visual content and a large audience: these are the characteristics of the most successful uses of the system. The ease with which up-to-date material and techniques can be conveyed to a large number of personnel is the major justification of the medium.

Demonstrations of equipment are particularly suited to this managed system: during the pre-production phase, the director and cameramen plan and practise shots of equipment in order to ensure good visibility. During the session, experts in its use can demonstrate its attributes and show procedures in close-up shots which, all in all, would be hard to replicate face-to-face at so many distributed sites. France Telecom project managers are well aware of the value of the visual component of their courses and exploit the potential of VIF for this kind of training.

Another valuable outcome of the use of VIF is that project managers responsible for training within the organization have become more involved in the actual process – by preparing sessions, introducing and attending broadcasts, and participating in live feedback about the session at the end of the day. Many have found this challenging and rewarding.

The centralization of training programmes brought about by the VIF system has the advantage of simplifying the logistics of large-scale training. For example, the demonstration of equipment at many sites used to require the transportation of many pieces from one location to another.

The CLR sites (one-way video; two-way audio) are considerably less interactive than the CLI sites, and as this makes some trainees feel excluded or at a disadvantage, most training uses are restricted to fully interactive sites.

Feedback shows that the training is least successful when the interests and level of experience of the trainees is very varied. It is better to run more sessions and keep the groups relatively homogeneous. Because each session ends with an evaluation period in which trainees comment on the usefulness of the training, early sessions in the programme can be used to refine later sessions.

On the whole, the financial costs of VIF sessions are roughly similar to face-to-face training. Occasionally where long distance travel and overnight stays are required, VIF does achieve cost savings. However, this was not the primary motivation for installing videoconferencing. (Permission for this case study has been given by France Telecom, and details were taken from Colbert *et al.*, 1993.)

References

Abbott, L, Dallat, J, Livingston, R and Robinson, A (1993) *Videoconferencing and Distance Learning*, Northern Ireland: University of Ulster.

Borbely, E (1993) 'Challenges and opportunities in extending the classroom and the campus via digital compressed video', in Mason, R and Bacsich, P (eds) *ISDN Applications in Education and Training*, London: Institution of Electrical Engineers.

Colbert, M, Voglimacci, C and Finklestein, A (1993) 'Use of Two "Live", Interactive, Audio-Visual Distance Learning Systems: Some experience and themes', University College London, manuscript.

Conboy, I (1993) 'MAX – an Australian approach to audiographics in schools', in Latchem, C, Williamson, J and Henderson-Lancett, L (eds), *Interactive Multimedia. Practice and Promise*, London: Kogan Page.

Idrus, R M (1992a) 'Technological innovation towards adult self-directed learning in the off-campus academic programme at the Universiti Sains Malaysia', *ICDE Bulletin*, **28**, 48–54.

Idrus, R M (1992b) 'Enhancing teletutorials via collaborative learning. The Malaysian experience', *DESOSNEWS*, **2**, 14.

Nordin, M R (1992) 'Workshop on audiographic teleconferencing at Universiti Sains Malaysia, 20–21 May 1991', *Open Learning*, June.

Owen, T (1993) 'Wired writing: The Writers in Electronic Residence program', in Mason, R (ed.) *Computer Conferencing: The last word*, Victoria, BC: Beach Holme Publishers.

Wells, R (1993) 'The use of computer-mediated communication in distance education: progress, problems and trends', in Davies, G and Samways, B (eds), *Teleteaching*, Amsterdam: North-Holland.

Witherspoon, J, Dozier, D and Harrison, P (1992) *An Initial Research Report: BESTNET applied to single-campus courses*, San Diego State University.

Chapter 8

Conclusions

Media choice

After much analysis of these three media, is there a conclusion about which medium to choose for education or training? In fact, most institutions never face an outright choice, as internal politics, financial considerations and educational needs usually dictate a technological direction. Champions of one medium or another commonly develop within organizations, and they have the energy and drive to promote their particular technology. For those educators who are in a position to make choices, it is first of all important to stress that there are no super-media. Quite the contrary; in fact, from the preceding discussion it should be obvious that each medium has unique benefits, but all have their drawbacks. Another way to look at media choice is to see that there is a role and a place for all of them – even in the same (albeit large) institution.

There are three important reasons why media are not 'in competition' with each other: students differ in their learning styles; the context of any technological innovation is paramount; and combinations of media are increasingly significant.

Learning Styles

The extensive research into learning styles has certainly established that people learn in different ways – in fact, so much so that it is a wonder that effective teaching ever takes place for more than a few learners on any one course. Structured learning opportunities are said to benefit certain types of students, while self-organized processes are preferred by others. There is the well-known divide between holistic and sequential (serialist) approaches to learning, and then there are visual, auditory or tactile learning preferences.

In terms of learners' perceptions of media, it is clear that many differences exist and, furthermore, these different perceptions affect the amount of mental effort the learner will make in engaging with material in any one form. The UK Open University has for years collected data from its students on their reactions to audiocassettes, video, television broadcasts and print:

I just can't learn from video; I need words in print.

I can't take in information from audio; I need to see something.

I've got to be able to see people in order to communicate with them.

These are typical of the range of comments from students about learning from various media. Consequently, there has been considerable support (not only at the UK OU) for presenting knowledge in a variety of different ways through a variety of media. Recasting theoretical issues into an audio discussion amongst experts, for instance, or visualizing complex explanations through computer simulation, or even putting into a printed table format the various points raised during an audiocassette discussion – all have been used to accommodate different learning styles.

Some institutions become locked into one medium and reinforce their stance by quoting feedback from students who excel with it. Just as there are media champions amongst the teaching staff, so there are amongst students, who have found a learning style which suits their needs. But what advantages one learner, may disadvantage another – at the critical level of understanding, before any questions of access or cost are even considered.

Context

Many of the apparently contradictory findings from research studies about various media can be resolved when considering the context of the application. Flexibility in learning time is an obvious case in point – its value to students overrides pedagogical considerations such as interactivity. Absence of any educational alternative makes most users of telecommunications technologies in remote or rural areas wildly enthusiastic about the advantages. However, for the face-to-face student asked to take some classes 'next door' to evaluate videoconferencing, a whole range of complaints and objections come to the surface:

You can't get as close to the tutors; the technology gets in the way.

It's difficult to pick up visual cues and body language.

It's hard to address the camera – there's no response. I felt constrained.

These are the kind of responses reported in studies where the students do not have a real need for the technology. Although a few applications of each of these media do facilitate activities or learning situations which could not take place face-to-face, on the whole, media are used to compensate for distance, to provide flexible study times or to support interactivity and contact with the tutor. When the student does not have one or more of these needs, the technology merely constrains rather than facilitates.

Combining Media

Although print material in the form of a study guide, set book or purpose-written units, is part of the learning strategy for most courses, an increasing number of courses are combining several technologies. This is proving effective for a number of reasons:

- computer technology supports a variety of media which combine well together: CD-Rom and text-based communications; electronic mail and computer-based training (CBT); access to remote databases and audiographics;
- technology-based combinations can make traditional face-to-face education more flexible (see case study 3 in Chapter 7 which combines video and computer conferencing);
- providing the students with a variety of media helps to satisfy a range of learning styles and circumstances.

In some cases, an expensive medium like videoconferencing is used sparingly with a less expensive medium like audiographics or computer conferencing providing a different kind of interaction or meeting other objectives of the course. Various kinds of combinations will become even more common when text, audio and video are integrated onto the desktop. Students will be able to concentrate on the medium which best suits their learning and communication style.

There are, of course, many teaching technologies other than the three communication media described here: a whole range of computer-based technologies, laser disks, stand-alone multimedia applications, and other communication tools, such as electronic mail and remote databases, as well as older technologies like audio and video cassettes. A wide range of combinations is possible which, used wisely, can help to educate the whole person, reaching the affective, social and cognitive domains.

There are choices to be made amongst the media, and this book has tried to inform the choice amongst three of them. Of course there must be an educational rationale for using any medium at all. What follows is a summary of the reasons for using communications media which have emerged from the previous chapters.

Educational Rationale

Access

Increasing the access to education and training is undoubtedly the primary benefit of introducing any communications technology. This may be for rural and isolated students, but it may equally well be for the cosmopolitan learner with no time to attend regular teaching sessions.

Equity

Providing equal educational opportunities for all is a wildly optimistic slogan, but elements of it are beginning to impinge on educators. Telecommunications offers some possibility of extending the benefits of educationally rich areas to the educationally disadvantaged.

It must be said, however, that while they increase access and equity for some, the use of communications technology widens still further the gap between the 'haves' and 'have-nots'.

Life-long learning

Telecommunications also offers the only possibility of providing life-long learning, professional updating, in-service training and community education – a cradle-to-the-grave provision which is independent of time and place. Networks, not buildings, are the educational future.

Sharing resources

Communications technologies facilitate the sharing of scarce resources, whether these resources are subject experts, digitized information or the experience of other students. Partnerships between education and industry, consortia of educational providers, cross-cultural institutional links, both national and international, and all joint initiatives to provide training and education are to be welcomed and encouraged by the use of communications media.

Interactivity

Interaction between learners and teachers has continually been shown to provide cognitive benefits, as well as to assist in the affective and motivational aspects of learning. Collaborative learning environments are known to foster many educationally desirable attributes: the active construction of knowledge, peer teaching and learning, and a self-directed approach to education. Demands from the workplace for cooperative work skills are beginning to have an effect in traditional education. Communications technologies can extend the practice of collaborative learning to students at a distance.

Close distance education

As they bridge the gap between traditional face-to-face education and traditional distance education, communications technologies have spawned a new term: 'close distance education'. It seems to encapsulate perfectly the advantages and disadvantages of these media.

The over-dependence on the lecture method may be a limitation of the traditional face-to-face teaching institutions, yet its parallel in distance education is the over-reliance on high-cost, purpose-produced print material. In order to amortize the cost of preparing and printing the material, the course must be delivered to large numbers of students for a long time. Not only is it difficult to mount courses quickly in response to student demand, but it is very difficult to maintain their currency in many areas of the curriculum.

Telecommunications offers an antidote both to the lecture and to the 'cast in concrete' course. By being at a 'close distance' to the institution, the teacher and the course material, students can hope to maintain their independence and flexibility while benefiting from the best of both worlds in educational provision.

Best practice in communications media

It is evident that there is 'no pleasing all the people all the time'. Nevertheless, some programmes are demonstrably better than others; some introductions of media into organizations are more successful than others, and some students can learn more and enjoy their learning more with some courses than with others.

The three components of success which emerge from this discussion are not medium-dependent. They are: course design, quality of teaching and support facilities. It is well accepted that people can learn from any medium and it is the way it is used which determines the learning outcomes. These three components are, nevertheless, dependent on a thorough understanding of the strengths and limitations of the particular medium used.

Course design

Good course design is a skill independent of any technological media. Elements include careful curriculum choice and a well-planned path through the content to meet the learning objectives. While the same principles of good course design apply to telecommunications courses, there are a few media-specific details which are critical.

With computer conferencing, they are: gauging the right conference size, devising a variety of student subgroupings and creating appropriate tasks for online collaboration. With audiographics, course design hinges on the appropriate balance between didactic presentation and group activities and interaction. This might require a reconception of the objectives and curriculum of a face-to-face delivered course. With videoconferencing, course design should involve the preparation of a whole range of visual material to support the course concepts.

Quality of teaching

It is often said that the telecommunications technologies show up a poor teacher more pointedly than face-to-face teaching. Good preparation beforehand and good communications skills over the medium are essential to successful telecommunications courses. The attitude of the teacher to the subject matter and to the students seems more evident than in face-to-face teaching – perhaps because students are more sensitized to it without the usual distractions. Much of the success of telecommunications so far is undoubtedly due to the enthusiasm and charisma of the teachers who have been attracted to using these media. Tips abound for each of the media, but in the last analysis it is usually acknowledged that teaching is an art, which some have naturally and others struggle to acquire.

Support facilities

Support facilities for students involve training in the use of the particular medium, but other aspects of the course also need support. For example, what facilities will be provided for library access; what arrangements will be made to deliver any print materials; will provisions be made for any face-to-face meetings; will a facilitator at each study centre or remote site be available; will the lecturer keep office hours for one-to-one contact; who will mark assignments and final examinations and how will feedback be provided to students? These kinds of support are secondary to the actual teaching, but they can make or break the educational experience.

Postscript

This book has tried to present a balanced overview of the use of three telecommunications media in education and training. The reader will easily find more enthusiastic and crusading literature on any one of them. The danger in analysing and evaluating any educational medium is that the spotlight of attention dazzles the viewers to the peccadilloes of everyday practice and activity in the wider world of education and training. How many students read all the written material of a course? How many carry out the in-text questions? What is the typical attention span in a face-to-face lecture? What are the attendance rates at lectures? What is the quality of discussion in face-to-face tutorials? What are the retention rates of face-to-face training? When the spotlight is turned on these practices, when students are asked for detailed feedback on the lecture system or the support system, on the quality of academic texts, journal articles or reading material, then the deficiencies of any one facility are seen in a different light.

Many institutions are using these three media in education and training. More would like to be. Hopefully the ideas and information here will help them to use these three technologies wisely.

Annotated bibliography

Computer conferencing

Keep, R (1991) *On-line. Electronic mail in the curriculum*, Coventry: National Council for Educational Technology.
This document is a comprehensive guide to the use of computer-mediated communication in UK schools. It covers the use of email for a whole range of purposes from developing language and intercultural understanding, to stimulating imagination in young users. It also contains a chapter on collecting and sharing database information. Written for the UK teacher, its section on costs, equipment and other practicalities may not have universal application, but the ideas and suggestions for using this technology certainly do.

Kaye, A R (ed.) (1992) *Collaborative Learning Through Computer Conferencing. The Najaden papers*, Berlin: Springer-Verlag.
This book looks at computer conferencing as a medium for cooperative work and analyses some of the main educational, social and technological issues. It contains contributions from users and implementers of conferencing systems in major universities and companies, from researchers and evaluators analysing the processes and outcomes of online group learning, and from software designers working on new systems for enhancing networked collaboration in groups.

Harasim, L (ed.) (1990) *Online Education. Perspectives on a new environment*, New York: Praeger.
Although this edited collection is intended to be theoretical in its approach,

it is very readable and contains a chapter by Roxanne Hiltz on her virtual classroom work. Those interested in the evaluation of conferencing applications will enjoy the chapter by Levin, Kim and Riel which includes their well known 'message map'.

Mason, R and Kaye, A R (eds) (1989) *Mindweave: communication, computers and distance education*, Oxford: Pergamon.
This volume (now out of print) is one of the earliest attempts to study the use of computer conferencing in distance education. The first section of eight chapters looks at themes and issues surrounding the use of this medium, and includes writings by the pioneers in the use of computer conferencing: Andrew Feenberg, Linda Harasim, Paul Levinson and Tony Kaye. The second section deals with the use of conferencing for mass distance education by the UK Open University. The last section contains 20 short papers taken from presentations and posters at the conference upon which the book was based.

Waggoner, M (ed.) (1992) *Empowering Networks. Computer conferencing in education*, Englewood Cliffs, NJ: Educational Technology Publications.
This is an edited collection of descriptive accounts, mostly American, of the use of computer conferencing in education. Examples range from tertiary education (eg, University of Michigan, the UK Open University) to primary/secondary applications (Big Sky Telegraph in Western Montana) to information resources (CompuServe). The last two chapters discuss barriers to the widespread acceptance of computer conferencing.

Wells, R (1992) *Computer-Mediated Communication for Distance Education: An international review of design, teaching, and institutional issues. ACSDE Research Monograph No. 6*, American Center for the Study of Distance Education, Pennsylvania State University.
This work is aimed at teachers, researchers and administrators interested in computer conferencing for distance education. It is set out in a very practical question and answer format and reviews the major questions and issues of the use of this medium. The last part of the monograph consists of a chart of educational and communications implementations.

Audiographics

Barker, B and Goodwin, R (1992) 'Audiographics: Linking remote classrooms', *The Computing Teacher*, April.

This is currently one of the best articles on audiographics use. It details the strengths and weaknesses of the medium and contains specific tips on effective teaching. The application which has provided the authors with such experience involves in-service training to teachers in Hawaii.

Conboy, I (1993) 'MAX – an Australian approach to audiographics in schools', in Latchem, C, Williamson, J and Henderson-Lancett, L (eds), *Interactive Multimedia. Practice and Promise*, London: Kogan Page.
By far the most detailed study of the introduction of audiographics into a school system, this account contains invaluable lessons and models of best practice. Extracts form the basis for case study 4 in Chapter 7.

Gunawardena, C (1992) 'Changing faculty roles for audiographics and online teaching', *American Journal of Distance Education*, **6**, 3, 58–71.
Writing from a teacher's perspective, Gunawardena describes her evolution from a teacher-led to student-centred approach due to her experience with audiographics and computer conferencing. This article is well worth reading on two counts: the interesting application of two technologies, and her self-analysis of the role of the teacher.

Knapczyk, D (1993) 'A distance-learning approach to in-service training', *EMI*, **30**, 2, 98–100.
This short article also outlines the use of audiographics for in-service teacher training, but is skills-based. The coursework is designed to improve the skills of school personnel who work with at-risk students in rural communities.

Smith, T (1992) 'The evolution of audiographics teleconferencing for continuing engineering education at the University of Wisconsin–Madison', *International Journal for Continuing Engineering Education*, **2**, 2/3/4, 155–160.
The University of Wisconsin has a long history of using telecommunications in distance education, particularly audiographics. This article details its use with small groups of professional engineers.

Videoconferencing

Abbott, L, Dallat, J, Livingston, R, and Robinson, A (1993) *Videoconferencing and Distance Learning*, Northern Ireland: University of Ulster.
This 1993 report follows on from a 1992 report entitled, *Videoconferencing and the Adult Learner*, and together they are a comprehensive evaluation of

the use of video at the University of Ulster. This application is unusual in that it is designed for small group, seminar-based learning – in this case for primary/secondary teachers. All the courses were evaluated both internally by the tutors and by an external researcher using questionnaires and interviews. This application is discussed in case study 7 in Chapter 7.

Atkinson, R, McBeath, C and Meacham, D (1991) *Quality in Distance Education. ASPESA Forum 91*, Lismore Heights, NSW: Australian and South Pacific External Studies Association.
This volume contains several papers on videoconferencing in Australia. Much of the factual information is now out of date, but it remains a useful book for institutions embarking on videoconferencing. Issues addressed include: implementation of video networks, students' perceptions, and growth of videoconferencing consortia.

Hansford, B and Baker, R (1990) 'Evaluation of a cross-campus interactive video teaching trial', *Distance Education*, **11**, 2.
Although this article is out of date by videoconferencing, and especially Australian videoconferencing standards, it provides a useful benchmark. Based on surveys of users and teachers, it gives a highly critical view of videoconferencing. This can be partly explained by the trial nature of the activity and the complete lack of training for the teachers. A comparison is made between the use of videoconferencing in large lectures and small groups.

Kristiansen, T (ed.) (1991) *A Window to the Future. The Videotelephone Experience in Norway*, Norwegian Telecom Research Department.
This short report is an excellent presentation of the use of videoconferencing by the Norwegian Telecom Research Department. The chapter on human factors issues in the design of the Norwegian videotelephone is interesting and well written, as are the three chapters on applications: supervision of habilitation and psychiatric work, teaching sign language and remote surveillance. The first two chapters on the development of the videotelephone and its relevance in distance education give the whole report a wide appeal.

Mason, R and Bacsich, P (eds) (1993) *ISDN Applications in Education and Training*, London: Institution of Electrical Engineers.
Although this book contains some specialist information about digital networks, the majority of chapters describe applications of videoconferencing and audiographics primarily in Europe, but also in Australia and North America. The emphasis is on the educational value of these technologies.

Phelan, A (1992) *DBS Pedagogical Scenarios. The use of direct broadcast satellite in the Multimedia Teleschool for European personnel development*, Dublin: Audio Visual Centre, University College.

This report is about the design and production of programmes to be broadcast by satellite on the DELTA-funded project, Multimedia TeleSchool. As these broadcasts are interactive, with live questions from students, the report has reviewed the issue of interactivity in higher education, as well as more general teaching and learning theory. These sections are very well presented and relevant to other interactive teaching media.

Pugh, L, Parchman, S and Simpson, H (1992) 'Video telecommunications for distance education: A field survey of systems in US public education, industry and the military', *Distance Education*, **13**, 2.

This field study of 13 US educational videoconferencing sites provides an excellent overview of different types and applications of the medium in America. Many of the systems described are used in training, and a mix of one-way and two-way video is chosen. Although feedback from users is consistently positive, poor quality audio is a common problem.

All three media

Burge, E and Roberts, J (1993) *Classrooms with a Difference. A practical guide to the use of conferencing technologies*. Toronto: Ontario Institute for Studies in Education.

This short manual presents four interactive technologies in the context of adult learning issues. It is written with an acknowledged bias towards humanistic traditions of education, and offers specific beliefs about technology and how it should be used. The focus throughout is on the holistic approach to learning in which technologies are subservient to theoretical principles. Highly recommended.

Davies, G and Samways, B (eds) (1993) *Teleteaching*, Proceedings of the IFIP TC3 Third Teleteaching Conference, Trondheim, Norway, Amsterdam: North-Holland.

This volume extends to nearly 1000 pages, but is very well presented as conference proceedings go. All of the papers involve the use of interactive technologies and altogether they provide the most up-to-date picture of the nature and extent of teleteaching worldwide. European examples are most numerous and many papers involve applications at school level. Some of the keynote papers at the beginning are excellent.

Moore, M (ed.) (1990) *Contemporary Issues in American Distance Education*, Oxford: Pergamon.
This collection of 32 papers is based upon a symposium on distance education held in 1988. Half a dozen papers are relevant to the area of telecommunications. Chute *et al.* present their research on 'learning from teletraining', which contains important conclusions about the appeal, acceptance and costs of various electronic media. Several papers focus on computer conferencing and others discuss videoconferencing.

Swift, M (1993) *Tele-Learning. A practical guide*, The Open Polytechnic of New Zealand.
This short guidebook is intended as an introduction and manual for users of the Tele-Learning Centre at the Open Polytechnic of New Zealand. Obviously much of the information is site- and country-specific; nevertheless, it provides a very basic introduction to computer communication, audiographics and videoconferencing, with detailed information and photographs of equipment. The review and explanation of different audio systems and microphones is particularly good, as is the section on audiographics software. The concept of tele-learning centres containing these facilities also provides an important model for good practice, which could be replicated in other countries. An excellent guide to the technical side of telematics.

Sources of information

Burge, E (1992) *Computer Mediated Communication and Education: A Selected Bibliography*, Toronto: Ontario Institute for Studies in Education.
This bibliography is set out both alphabetically and by topic such as learner perspective, tutor/moderator perspective, education issues, tools and techniques. It centres on the medium of computer conferencing in higher education. It contains many early references as well as being comprehensive up until April 1992.

ICDL Distance Education Database (available online and CD-Rom). International Centre for Distance Learning, Open University.

DEOSNEWS (Distance Education Online Symposium). Electronic

Journal. To subscribe: send email to listserv@psuvm.edu with the message subscribe DEOSNEWS <your name>

Journals: *Open Learning*, Longman Group, UK.
Distance Education, Darling Downs Institute Press, Queensland, Australia.
American Journal of Distance Education, Pennsylvania State University, USA.
Interactive Teaching Technology, Wiley, UK.
Educational and Training Technology International, Kogan Page, UK.

Glossary

analogue	Information represented by a continuous electrical signal whose strength depends on the signal received from a sound or light source.
asynchronous	In education, asynchronous interaction is where two or more parties are not present at the same time.
audiobridge	A method of connecting a small number of telephone lines, and equalizing noise distortion and background noise for a live audioconference.
audiographics	A small range of technologies which combine a live voice link with a shared screen for computer graphics, real-time drawing or pre-prepared material to link together two or more sites.
bandwidth	The range of frequencies required to transmit a signal. For example, voice over the telephone network requires a bandwidth of 3kHz while uncompressed video requires a bandwidth of 6 mHz.
cable television	A broadband distribution network, using coaxial or fibre-optic transmission technology, which carries multiple television channels to domestic and business subscribers within an urban franchise area. Cable television networks can also carry telephony and information services.
CCITT	Consultative Committee on International Tele-

	phony and Telegraphy. An international standards group.
CODEC	COder-DECoder. Converts analogue data into a digital signal for transmission and re-converts after reception. Two CODECs are required, one at each end of a channel.
compressed video	Processing technique to reduce the bandwidth required to transmit video frames over a tele-communications channel. This results in a reduction in transmission time, therefore a reduction in cost.
computer conferencing	A development of electronic mail designed for effective support of many-to-many communication. Conferencing software includes features specifically designed to help in the organization, structuring and retrieval of messages. Messages can be linked to each other as comments and organized in different branches or topics. Special commands are available to the person responsible for a conference (called the moderator), which can help in defining the membership of the conference, in keeping the discussion on track, and in scheduling the opening and closing of discussion topics.
digital	The representation of data or physical quantities by means of digits (discrete elements).
distribution list	A facility in electronc mail systems to enable a large number of subscriber mail addresses to be reached through a single (list) name.
electronic mail	Often abbreviated to email, a system of electronic communication whereby an individual sends a message to another individual or group of people.
facsimile	Almost always referred to as 'fax', a technique for transmitting text and black-and-white pictures over the telephone network.
full duplex	A telecommunications channel which allows conversation to take place interactively and simultaneously between the various parties without electronically cutting off one or more participants if someone else is speaking.

half duplex	A telecommunications channel which allows conversation to take place in only one direction at a time.
image bank	A local area or wide area network resource containing a large number of still pictures and motion video clips, stored in compressed digital or analogue form, and accessible through an associated database of descriptive information.
interface	In terms of the user, the way in which a system such as a piece of software presents itself. For example, modern software systems present themselves with a graphical user interface consisting of information in windows.
Internet	The inter-operating collection of academic computer networks which link most universities and other organizations into a worldwide 'web' or 'meta-network'.
ISDN	Integrated Services Digital Network is a set of international switching standards to which worldwide telecommunications providers are recommended to adhere. However, to date there is no universal agreement to the standards. As an integrated digital network, it can be used for more than one service, such as telephony and data transfer.
kbits/s	A digital data rate expressed in 1/1000s of bits per second.
leased lines	The rented use of a dedicated circuit which runs from one point to another. They can be analogue or digital, and can use fibre optics, telephone lines, microwave or other transmission systems.
light pen	A pen-like device that can be used to 'write' directly on a computer screen. It can be used to write freehand on the screen, to interact with a menu/windowing system on the screen and to enter and edit graphics.
mbits/s	A digital data rate expressed in millions of bits per second.
modem	MOdulator/DEModulator. A device used to connect computers via an analogue telephone line.

	It converts digital computer data into an analogue signal and back again.
multimedia	The use of several media (text, diagram, image, audio or video), which can be accessed randomly and non-sequentially.
online	A system is operating online if it is connected to a remote system. Thus a microcomputer is online if it is connected to a remote computer system (such as a database or a computer conferencing system).
resource-based learning	The use of educational resources (films, videos, textbooks, CBT sofware packages, computer databases, etc.) to facilitate learning, especially of a self-directed nature. In order that resources are available electronically, a massive amount of digitization has to take place and there are major problems such as copyright to be overcome.
scanner	A device for digitizing text, drawings or photographs (anything in paper form). It works like a photocopy machine, except that the scanner converts the printed image into digital images that can be manipulated by computer software packages.
synchronous	In education, synchronous interaction is where two or more parties are present at the same time, though not necessarily in the same place.
telepresence	In teleconferencing situations, the use of communications technology to provide each user with the feeling that the users at other sites are physically present.
videoconferencing	The combination of audio and visual media to provide interactive communication between two or more sites.
video window	A method of displaying motion television, usually by means of an additional hardware board, within a selected portion (window) of a personal computer screen. It is used in multimedia to display moving images from analogue video disk, and in live desktop conferencing to show participants at other network locations.

voicemail	A system that records voice messages in the original voice of the caller.
VSAT	Very Small Aperture Terminal. A satellite system for voice, data or video where the satellite dish is less than about 3 metres in diameter.

Index